MACRAME

FOR BEGINNERS

Discover How To Easily Start Your Macramé Activity

With Many Different Easy DIY Projects

Ashley Cotton

MACRAME FOR BEGINNERS

TABLE OF CONTENTS

Introduction

Macramé is a kind of textile made using multiple knots. With macramé, you can complete a project by simply using your hands and a mounting ring to hold your piece steady as you work. So how did macramé come about?

History of Macrame

Recently, there has been a craze for macramé; however, this is not its first appearance. Macramé was first adapted by the Arabic countries around the 13th century. Weavers from this area used different types of knotting techniques to create rugs and shawls. Further, creating decorative pieces like wall hangings using knots can also be traced back to third-century China.

Thanks to the Arabic artisans, macramé spread through Europe. The practice had spread as far as England by the late seventeenth century, where Queen Mary II, ladies in waiting adapted the craft.

The beauty of macramé was that it was not practiced by women only; sailors knotted as well for practical reasons. However, when they embarked on drawn-out voyages, knotting worked as a method of warding off boredom and staying engaged, which ultimately aided in spreading the art all through Europe. When they docked on new ports, they turned to merchants and traded out the macramé designs they had been making through their voyage. Some common pieces included belts, hammocks, and hats.

Eventually, in the eighteenth and nineteenth centuries, Victorians would knot textiles until the Industrial Revolution when sewing machines overtook the practice. However, during the late 1960s and 1970s, hand-knotting made a comeback, but by the 1980s, it quickly fell out of fashion.

With that out of the way, let us now see how you stand to benefit by learning macramé.

The Benefits of Learning Macramé

Learning the art of macramé is great because it offers you several great benefits. Here are some of the top reasons why you should try macramé.

It Makes You More Creative

Macramé knots are similar to building Lego blocks; as soon as you identify how to tie them, you can assemble them in wonderful patterns through great ease. Being able to arrange those knots without the aid of any prepared designs or patterns can open up your mind imaginatively. Everyone is creative; all you need is to trust and believe in yourself to reveal that part of your brain. You are free to express yourself in what you make, and therefore this allows you to engage your creative side and make breathtaking macramé pieces.

It Helps You Grow

The art of macramé is great because just like any other art, it is a delightful method to meet individuals and study more about the creation round you. It motivates you to get out of your comfort zone and try new interesting skills. It challenges your thinking and makes you become better. Once you are out of your comfort zone, growing with each day, you start to grow and become a better person. Learning macramé allows you to live an active, healthy, and connected life, as you spend time learning what other people are doing, get inspired by their crafts, find ways of improving or customizing them, and more.

It Gives You Time and Permission to Learn A New Skill

People are always looking to learn new beneficial skills. By learning macramé, you build a new skill that is not only fun but also very beneficial to you. It is always challenging to try something new because you're not used to the change. Therefore, to make it more interesting and fun, you need to try something that challenges you while at the same time being interesting. Macramé offers just that – the perfect combination of challenges and fun as you slowly become better knot by knot. Once you create something nice, you'll feel quite happy and satisfied that you'll love engaging in macramé.

It Allows You to Make Amazing Works of Art

Macramé is a great form of art that allows you to create beautiful works of art. There are many things that you can make from macramé, such as wall hangings, jewelry, clothes, or even sandals. Being able to create something just the way you want it is good because you'll be satisfied and content with it.

These amazing works of art can be used to decorate homes or even offices. They add a great touch to the vibe and general look of a place. You could even gift your loved ones and impress them with your skills and thoughtfulness.

It Is A Way to Make A Living Easily

If you've been looking for a way to make a living by doing your own business, then macramé is the way to go. People are always looking for ways to decorate their offices and homes. And with the fact that you can create unique pieces that inspire and ooze elegance, you could easily sell your crafts to people. People love beautiful things, irrespective of how the economy is performing! So, if you can perfect this skill, you could make it your little side hustle, which could easily pay some bills for you. And if you are serious about it and become a pro at macramé, you could even turn it into a full-time business, as you make breathtaking works of art that people will not say no to.

CHAPTER 1
How to Get Started to Macrame – The Basic Knots

We will introduce you to some fundamental Macramé knots prior to actually going right into the ventures. It will be the main pillar of Macramé lessons. Furthermore, it will assist you to improve faster through each of the ventures that we will be going through. Generally, there are five specific Macramé knots that you ought to know – both within. You are committed to developing some lovely Macramé items if you focus on making those knots. What you will start finding with these mentioned Macramé knots is that most of the Macramé designs would use one or all of these knots. You will be able to simply get through every Macramé project by trying to learn these simple yet important knots. Furthermore, it will allow you to customize some knots to build your own exclusive Macramé pattern. The five baseline Macramé knots include:

- Lark's Head Knot

- Square Knot

- Berry Knot

- Gathering Knot Double half hitch knot

The above-mentioned knots will be the strings you need to utilize the most often. These are the beginning and finishing ties that you will be incorporating on several of the things you are doing. There are tons of knots you will want to learn, for sure. However, these ties are a decent building block for moving you on the correct track. In case you are not yet acquainted with these five ties, it is suggested that you exercise doing them up several times before you are comfortable with the technique of connecting.

Different Methods of Tying a Knot

Learn how to tie these basic knots off by core, as they are repeatedly utilized.

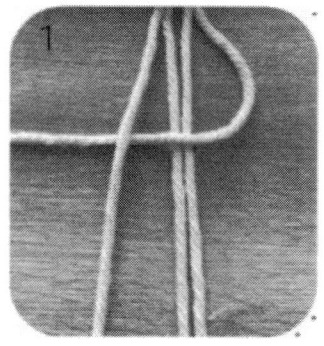 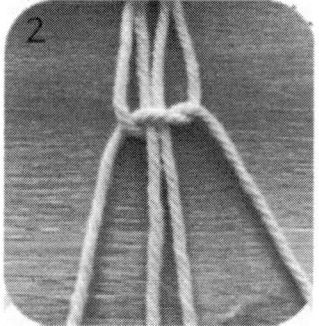

Reef Knot (Square)

This is utilized to connect two cord ends of even density and can be loosened by pulling one end back over the knot if needed. It is the foundation in macramé for the square knot.

1. Split cords and lay beside each other so that the two shorter (core) cords are in the center.
   * carry the right cord underneath the fundamental cords and over the left cord.

2. Take the cord at the leftover of the core cords and transfer it through the loop at the right. Pull the cords to get the knot firm. Repeat from * until the duration needed is in the spiral. To break the loop, adjust the path you tie the knot to.

Square Knot Forms

The square knot is a successful knot used to make macramé bracelets and other paracord items, and the consequent flat knot braid is regarded as Solomon bar. You can deal with new ways to manipulate the simple square knot to produce many appealing variations.

Crossed Cords

To produce a cross-stitch effect, apply a contrast cord color to the base square knot cords, with a flowing stitch design on the reverse side.

1. Begin with an overhand knot and operate one square knot; feed the ends of a variation cord color under the core cords, until you secure the knot.
2. Pass the right-hand comparison chord over the left and lower the key cords to each side of the ears.
3. Perform the first half of the next square knot: left cord underneath the core cords, right cord over the core cords, and bottom through the loop on the left.
4. 4Raise up the cords in comparison over the knots. Perform the second half of the square tie, and then take the correct cord under the contrast cords but over the center cords and the wrong cord. Taking the chord on the left under the contrast cords, through the core cords and Bottom into the loop on the right.
5. Repeat measures 2–4 starting with a cross template. Each time, you can switch the right cord over the left, or alternate for another impact.

Woven Knot Square

Working over the four basic strands, this creates a twisted look Bottom the center of the braid. Ignore the stage directions closely, since each time the cords are not connected like a simple square knot.

1. Knead and rotate a knot overhand. * Bring the left chord above the left core line, behind the right core chord and over the right line. Move the correct cord under both cords as seen, and up through the left cable. Pull ends up the standing firm.

2. Place the right cord under the right core cord, over the left core cord, and below the left cord. Then under all cords, take the left-hand cord and up through the right loop.

3. Continue to repeat from * until braid has the required length. To finish the task, tie a standard knot in the square.

Overhand Knot

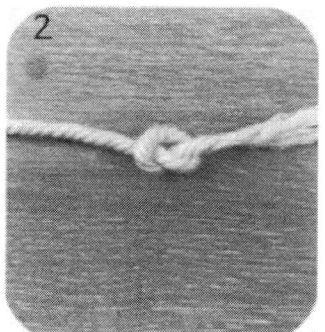

This basic knot may be attached as a stopper at the end of a rope or as a reminder of the beginning point, or it can be used to detach or connect beads, or simply to create a slipping fastener. Working over the thumb, create a loop in the clockwise direction and, through the loop, pull the working thread up.

Slip Knot

The slipknot is tied to the base of many knotted braids so that the working end is adjustable. Create an anticlockwise loop and keep the string in your left hand at the cross point (below). Place the working cord behind the string, and draw into a U-shaped curve. To change the loop scale, pull the short beginning finish to secure the tie and the working edge.

Lark's Head Knot

This knot is used to tie one cord to another, or to connect a cord to a bar or ring as seen here, and is the most commonly used knot for macramé projects to launch. Split one cord in half, and go around the loop you built from front to back around the pipe. Move the rope around the tails and drawback to close. To create a head knot of a reverse lark, move the rope on the reverse side through the ring and complete the knot again by moving the tails through the circle.

Half-Hitch Knot

One of the foundational macramé knots, like shown here, is worked over another cord, or over a ring or bar. It is also used to hold finer cords or threads in pairs. To make a half hitch, take one cord and pass the working end under the other cord and behind the start end. Create a second loop in the same direction around the loop between both the two half hitches to move the job end for extra protection.

Carrick Bend Knot

This knot can be worked on two cords or Utilizing just one thread as explained and it is the basis of many ornamental knots. Start making a loop in one cord in the clockwise direction with the tails on left. Toss the second cord at the bottom right behind the loop, with the starting end. Transfer the working end below the first cord's tails then sew it over and below the cords to come out again at the top of the right loop.

Utilizing Basic Knots

The easiest ties will create the most exquisite jewelry. Overhand knots can be tied to separate or connect beads, and Overhand knots can be connected separately or add beads and reef knots to create a simple and easy bracelet, and there are even other ideas in this segment to bring the best out of common knots.

Overhand Knots

The overhand knot looks awesome wrapped in a rustic leather cord; it can be used for removing beads and adding charms, and for a quick slipping fastening.

1. Use overhand knots to anchor a bead on cord lengths or space beads along leather lengths. Select the cord that correlates to the depth of the bead cavity.
2. One of the strands may be thinner when constructed for two or three cord strands to move through small-hole beads before connecting all the strands together with an overhand knot.
3. Utilize an overhand knot to fasten a charm hop ring or chain around the cord circumference. Bind the knot to the same side of the chain by links to prevent it from twisting.
4. Loop two cord lengths in opposite directions via a washer style bead or button, and then tie each side with an overhand knot to secure it.
5. Make a small beaded tassel by tying a bunch of cords with an overhand knot; add a bead to each strand and tie an overhand knot to secure it above and below the knot.
6. Rest two cords in opposite directions for a sliding fastening and tie an overhand knot over the other cord at each end and firm each. Pull open the tails, and close the main cord.

Reef Knot

Cord too thick for tying intricate knots when working a reef knot can be converted into an easy and efficient design, desirable for making a pretty bracelet.

1. Break two 6 mm chord lengths of 25 cm (10 in), and make a knot of the coral. Change the knot to the same duration on both sides, and softly tug to tighten up.
2. Test the bracelet duration for the fastening, trim the ends of the rope, and fasten all cords to the fastening at either end utilizing solid jewelry glue.

The Head-Knot of Lark

Sometimes forgotten, this is one of the most popular knots to create jewelry and accessories-the head knots of single or several larks may be used to construct beautiful jewelry designs. In a slide fastening ready to operate a large panel of macramé to create a cuff necklace, the Tie lark's head twists around the loops. Utilizing the head knot of the lark to tie a rope to a sturdy ring to create a pendant, which can be further embellished with bead charms and hop rings. Secure a loop, or another type, with the head knot of a lark on either hand and then secure the ends for a simple bracelet in a fastener.

Nesting Lark's Head Knot

The head knot of the nesting lark is useful when tangling or working macramé, utilize two cord color schemes. Fasten the head knot of a lark with the first cord (light pink), then lay the second cord (dark pink) laterally under the first knot, take the ends around the back of the base cord and tuck into the created loop.

Multiple Lark Head's Knots

Continue to work the knots one after the other uses a bit distinct methodology, as you will have to stitch one tail across the core cord in order to make the head knot of a lark follow the correct path.

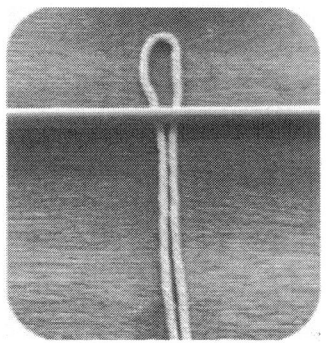  

Single-Core Technique

1. Use the head knot of a lark to attach a thin cord to one end of a thicker core cord; tie on a second length of thin cord with the head knot of a lark facing in the opposite direction.

2. Work a half hitch over the core cord with the first working-end. Move the job end once more under the core cord and back up through the rope to complete the head knot of a third lark.

3. Start moving from side to side with alternating strings, doing the head knot of one lark at a time. Beads can be inserted Bottom each side of the large loops.

Double Core Technique

1. For the size of a bracelet: tie the head knot of a lark in the center of a thick leather cord that is 40 cm (16 in) wide. Bend this core cord in half, and take over and over the other half of the core cord the top working cord of the lark's head knot.

2. Create a second lark's head knot as Single Core Procedure on the right side of the rope, stage 2, and then diagonally move the right-hand working cord around and over the left-hand heart. Wear the head-knot of a lark. Take the working cord on the left through and over the core cord on the right. Tie the head knot of another larynx.

3. Proceed the crisscross sequence of the head-knots of the lark all the way back Bottom the core cords. The structure of the top loop can be adjusted to fit a button or toggle.

CHAPTER 2

Beginner Guide to Macrame Cord and Metal Shapes Selecting

Macramé stylists make use of different types of materials. The materials can be classified in two major ways; the natural materials and the synthetic materials.

Natural Materials

The qualities of natural materials differ from the synthetic material and knowing these qualities would help you to make better use of them. Natural cord materials existing today include Jute, Hemp, Leather, Cotton, Silk and Flax. There are also yarns made from natural fibers. Natural material fibers are made from plants and animals.

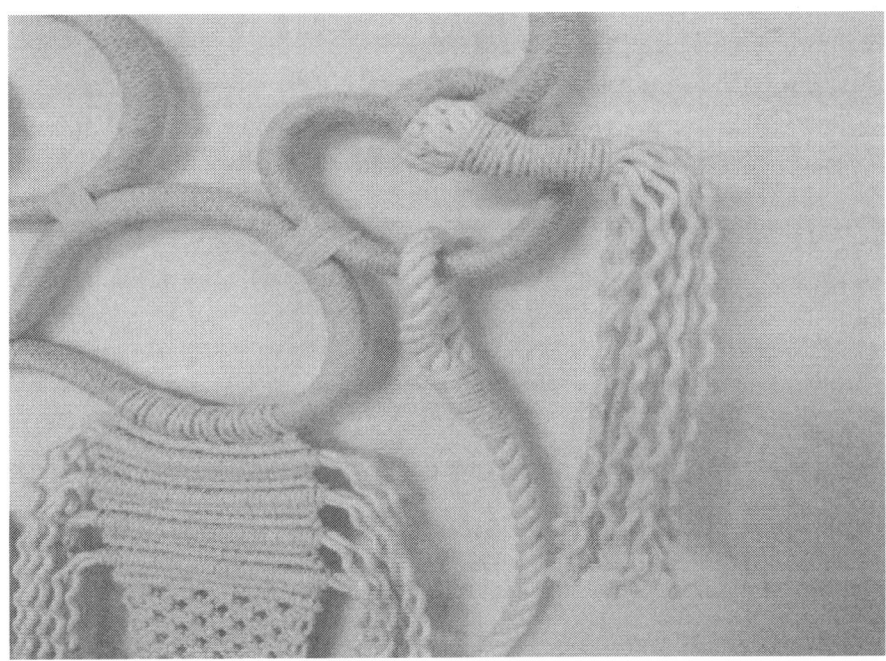

Synthetic Materials

Like natural materials, synthetic materials are also used in macramé projects. The fibers of synthetic materials are made through chemical processes. The major ones are nylon beading cord, olefin, satin cord and parachute cord.

Cord Measurement

Before you can embark on a macramé project, it is essential that you determine the amount of chord you will need. This includes knowing the length of the required cord and the total number of materials you have to purchase.

Equipment: to measure, you will need a paper for writing, pencil, tape rule and calculator. You would also need some basic knowledge of unit conversion as shared below:

1 inch = 25.4millimeters = 2.54 centimeters

1 foot =12 inches

1 yard = 3 feet = 36 inches

1 yard = 0.9 meters

Note: The circumference of a ring = 3.14 * diameter measured across the ring

Measuring Width

The first thing to do is determine the finished width of the widest area of your project. Once you have this width, pencil it down.

Determine the actual size of the materials, by measuring its width from edge to edge.

You can then proceed to determine the type of knot pattern you wish to use with the knowledge of the knot pattern. You must know the width and spacing (if required) of each knot. You should also determine if you want to add more cords to widen an area of if you would be needing extra cords for damps.

With the formula given above, calculate and determine the circumference of the ring of your designs.

Determine the mounting technique to be used. The cord can be mounted to a dowel, ring or other cord. Folded cords affect both the length and width of the cord measurement.

Cord Preparation

Though usually rarely emphasized, preparation of the cords and getting them ready for use in Macramé projects is one of the core pillars of the art of Macramé. At times, specialized processes such as conditioning and stiffening of cords need to be carried out before Macramé projects can be begun. In general, however, cord preparation in Macramé is mainly concerned with dealing with cut ends and preventing these ends from unraveling during the course of the project. During the course of a project, constant handing of materials can cause distortion in the ends which can end up having disastrous consequences on your project. Before starting your project, if you do not appropriately prepare special kinds of cords, like ones that were made by the twisting of individual strands, that cord is likely to come apart, effectively destroying your project completely Therefore, cord preparation is extremely and incomparably important to the success of any Macramé project, the preparation of each cord is meant to be done during the first step of making any knot, which is the step where you cut out your desired length of cord from the larger piece.

For cord conditioning, experts recommend rubbing beeswax along the length of the cord. To condition your cord, simply get a bit of beeswax, let it warm up a bit in your hands, and rub it along the cord's length. This will help prevent unwanted tight curls on your cord. Note that beeswax may be applied to both natural and synthetic materials. For synthetic materials however, only Satin and fine Nylon beading cords actually compulsorily require conditioning. After conditioning, inspect your cords for any imperfections and discard useless pieces to ensure the perfection of your project. After conditioning, then comes the actual process of cord preparation. Cords can be prepared (i.e., the ends can be prevented from fraying) through the use of a flame, a knot, tape and glue.

To prevent unraveling of your cord using a flame, firstly test a small piece of the material with the flame from a small lighter. The material needs to melt, not burn. If it burns, then such a cord is not suitable for flame preparation. To prepare using a flame, simply hold the cord to the tip of the flame for 2 to 5 seconds, make sure the cord does not ignite, but melts. Flame preparation is suitable for cords made from olefin, polyester and nylon, and the process is compulsory for the preparation of parachute cords. The overhand knot is an all-time favorite, but knots such as the figure 8 knot which is best suited to flexible cords can be used if you think the knot might have to be undone at some point of your project. The Stevedore knot can be used to prevent fraying when using slippery materials. Glue is another priceless alternative that can be used to prevent fraying at the ends of cords efficiently. However, not all kinds of glue may be used in cord preparation. Only certain brands, such as the Aleen's Stop Fray may be used in cord preparation. Household glue might also be used, but only when diluted with water. TO prepare your cord, simply rub the glue on the ends of the material and leave it to dry. If you intend to pass beads over the glued end, roll the cord's end between your fingers to make it narrower as it dries. Nail polish may also be used as an alternative to glue. A special class of Macramé cords, known as a parachute cord, requires a special form of preparation. Parachute cords are composed of multiple core yarns surrounded by a braided sleeve. To prepare a parachute cord (also called a Paracord), pull out the core yarns from the sleeve, and expose the yarns by about half an inch. Now cut the core yarns back, so that they become even with the outer sleeve, and then push the sleeve forward till the yarns become invisible.

To complete the preparation, apply flame to the outer sleeve till it melts, and then press the handle of your lighter onto the sleeve while it's still warm to flatten the area and keep it closed up. The melted area will look darker and more plastic than the rest of the material.

Finishing Techniques

Finishing techniques refer to the methods by which the ends of cords, after knots have been created may be taken care of to give a neat and tidy project. Finishing is often referred to as tying off. Several finishing knots are available and are extremely effective methods for executing finishing processes. Reliable finishing knots include the overhand knot and the barrel knot.

Folding techniques are also dependable finishing techniques. For flexible materials like cotton, all you need to do is fold the ends flat against the back surface and add glue to the ends to hold them in place. For less flexible materials, fold the cords to the back, then pass them under a loop from one or more knots, and then apply glue, allow it to dry, and cut off excess material.

Finally, you can do your finishing with the aid of fringes. You may choose between a brushed fringe and a beaded fringe.

Adding Cords

During Macramé projects, you would constantly be faced by the need to add a cord to an existing cord or any other surface such as a ring or a dowel. The process of adding cords to surfaces is usually called mounting. To add extra cords to a ring or dowel, the most common technique to use is the Reverse Larks Head Knot. When adding cords to already existing cords in use, however, it is important that the new cords blend into the overall design. To prevent lopsidedness of the pattern, it is also important to add an equal number of cords to both sides in some projects. It is also important to avoid gaps when adding new cords. You can add new cords to an already existing cord using the square knot, the linked overhand knot and of course the regular overhand knot. Other techniques used for adding cords include the diamond stitch and the triangle knot.

CHAPTER 3
Training Before Starting

Picking Materials and Prepping Your Workspace

Decide on the kind of string you'll need depending on your task. There are such huge numbers of kinds of strings you can use for macramé. Just use cotton for the rope, yarn, twine, cowhide, or whatever else that arrives in an effectively flexible strand. Cowhide is incredible in case you're making gems. Cotton rope functions admirably in case you're making a wall hanging, and you can use yarn to make a scarf or cover.

Collect a couple of sewing pins. Contingent upon the knots you'll be using, you may need pins to hold your tying material off the beaten path. Sewing pins are an incredible choice for this. You can likewise use thumbtacks.

Make a task board. This doesn't need to be anything extravagant, simply something compact, however delicate enough to push sticks through. You can stick a nursery stooping cushion or an old soap resting cushion to a clipboard. You can likewise use balsa wood or Styrofoam. Pick a stay. The stay is the bit of metal, wood, or plastic that you join your tying material. You'll set it at the highest point of your job board and use it to assemble your task. Your stays will change contingent upon the venture. In case you're making adornments or a keychain, a keyring is likely best. For bigger tasks, a dowel or a bar will function admirably. Beginning Your Project with a Reverse Lark's Head Knot crease your line into equal parts. You'll need to ensure that your overlay is actually half. You'll be using the remainder of this line for different knots, and if it's lopsided, it may influence the remainder of your project. Place the circle under your stay. Place the circle shaped by collapsing the string into equal parts under the dowel or pole with the 2 parts of the deals above. In case you're using a ring, place the circle under one side of the ring, so the circle is in the center. Pull the circle up and the lines down through it. Pull the circle over the bar, dowel, or at the edge of the ring. Stay put your finger up through the circle and hold the two parts of the string. Pull them down through the circle. The circle and lines should make a pretzel shape.

Pull down on the line to make the knot tight. Hold the bar, dowel, or ring with 1 hand. With the other, pull down on the 2 parts of the rope. As you do, the circle will climb toward the bar, dowel, or ring, pulling the knot tight. Set up various strings for new tasks. Most macramé ventures will require in any event 2 groups of tying strings. Thus, you will need to tie at least 2 converse lark's head knots, with 2 bits of macramé rope, on a similar stay, to begin any project.

Cord Preparation

Though usually rarely emphasized, preparation of the cords and getting them ready for use in Macramé projects is one of the core pillars of the art of Macramé. At times, specialized processes such as conditioning and stiffening of cords need to be carried out before Macramé projects can be begun. In general, however, cord preparation in Macramé is mainly concerned with dealing with cut ends and preventing these ends from unraveling during the course of the project. During the course of a project, constant handing of materials can cause distortion in the ends, which can end up having disastrous consequences on your project. Before starting your project, if you do not appropriately prepare special kinds of cords, like ones that were made by the twisting of individual strands, that cord is likely to completely come apart, effectively destroying your project.

Therefore, cord preparation is extremely and incomparably important to the success of any Macramé project, the preparation of each cord is meant to be done during the first step of making any knot, which is the step where you cut out your desired length of cord from the larger piece.

For cord conditioning, experts recommend rubbing beeswax along the length of the cord. To condition your cord, simply get a bit of beeswax, let it warm up a bit in your hands, and rub it along the cord's length. This will help prevent unwanted tight curls on your cord. Note that beeswax may be applied to both natural and synthetic materials. However, for synthetic materials, only Satin and fine Nylon beading cords actually compulsorily require conditioning. After conditioning, inspect your cords for any imperfections and discard useless pieces to ensure the perfection of your project. After conditioning, then comes the actual process of cord preparation. Cords can be prepared (i.e., the ends can be prevented from fraying) through the use of a flame, a knot, tape, and glue.

To prevent unraveling of your cord using a flame, firstly test a small piece of the material with the flame from a small lighter. The material needs to melt, not burn. If it burns, then such a cord is not suitable for flame preparation. To prepare using a flame, simply hold the cord to the tip of the flame for 2 to 5 seconds, make sure the cord does not ignite but melts. Flame preparation is suitable for cords made from olefin, polyester, and nylon, and the process is compulsory for the preparation of parachute cords.

Tying knots at the end of the cord is another effective method to prevent fraying. The overhand knot is an all-time favorite, but knots such as the figure 8 knot, which is best suited to flexible cords, can be used if you think the knot might have to be undone at some point in your project. The Stevedore knot can be used to prevent fraying when using slippery materials.

Glue is another priceless alternative that can be used to efficiently prevent fraying at the ends of cords. However, not all kinds of glue may be used in cord preparation. Only certain brands, such as Aleen's Stop Fray may be used in cord preparation. Household glue might also be used, but only when diluted with water. TO prepare your cord, simply rub the glue on the ends of the material and leave it to dry. If you intend to pass beads over the glued end, roll the cord's end between your fingers to make it narrower as it dries. Nail polish may also be used as an alternative to glue.

The tape is also a reliable method to prepare your cords. Simply wrap the tape around the end of the cord where you want to prevent the fraying of your material. Make sure the end of the cord remains narrow by squeezing it between your fingers. It is advisable to use masking tape or cellophane tape for your preparations.

A special class of Macramé cords, known as a parachute cord, requires a special form of preparation. Parachute cords are composed of multiple core yarns surrounded by a braided sleeve. To prepare a parachute cord (also called a Paracord), pull out the core yarns from the sleeve, and expose the yarns by about half an inch. Now cut the core yarns back so that they become even with the outer sleeve, and then push the sleeve forward till the yarns become invisible. To complete the preparation, apply flame to the outer sleeve till it melts, and then press the handle of your lighter onto the sleeve while it's still warm to flatten the area and keep it closed up. The melted area will look darker and more plastic than the rest of the material.

Finishing Techniques

Finishing techniques refer to the methods by which the ends of cords after knots have been created, may be taken care of to give a neat and tidy project. Finishing is often referred to as tying off.

Several finishing knots are available and are extremely effective methods for executing finishing processes. Reliable finishing knots include the overhand knot and the barrel knot.

Folding techniques are also dependable finishing techniques. For flexible materials like cotton, all you need to do is fold the ends flat against the back surface and add glue to the ends to hold them in place. For less flexible materials, fold the cords to the back, then pass them under a loop from one or more knots, and then apply glue, allow it to dry, and cut off excess material. Finally, you can do your finishing with the aid of fringes. You may choose between a brushed fringe and a beaded fringe.

CHAPTER 4
Macrame Important Tips and Tricks

It's such an amazing feeling to discover macramé and get inspired to learn, but it can also be daunting when you sit down and trying to figure out how to start.

Begin with Simple Knots

There are too many different knots to know if you're new to the game, which can seem overwhelming. To get the methodology down, we recommend you begin with a few simple patterns and knots.

A decent first to know knot is a basic knot in a rectangle. These days, this knot is the very foundation of much of the macramé out there, and a surprisingly simple knot for beginners to try. This knot is the one all learn in our workshops!

Attend A Workshop

Educating yourself is enjoyable, but I recommend you attend a workshop if you have any in your city. You get to interact with too many like-minded individuals and also depart not just with your own finished artwork but even with new mates.

Save Your Left-Over Chord

As you're practicing, there might be a handful of attempts you're going to fight back. And getting the right JUST rope length can be your biggest barrier. You never want to have little rope because attaching extra to your piece can be complicated. We also recommend that you make at least 10 percent more errors than you think you should, just to be healthy. We have a comprehensive step-by-step calculation in the latest Modern Macramé book on how to decide how much rope you need for your macramé! This is in mind; at the end of your project, maybe you wind up with extra rope! But don't think! We suggest that you save every rope leftover. You should recycle the recycled rope into potential designs.

Study Online

If you can't see us at a laboratory in person, viewing videos online is the second-best thing. Often, it's easier to follow someone who shows you the ropes, rather than reading instructions on a page. There are many tutorials on YouTube.

Have Fun

One of the best aspects of the trip is sharing your imagination through Macramé! Don't be too hard on yourself. T Let your imagination take the lead, and you'll end up with a beautiful product.

Macramé Supplies

To build the craft projects, Macramé supplies and crafts equipment is required. There is a list of the specific things that you need below before beginning any project. Many markets and hardware stores hold stocks of art if you don't have such things at home already. You should have a table or some other surface to function. Working far from home on your idea, a clipboard will keep the ropes but also offers you a solid surface to operate on. The ropes used during Macramé are often very long, so when they become caught in them, they can hurt pets so small children. Seek to bring all your resources into some sort of quick to transport organizer.

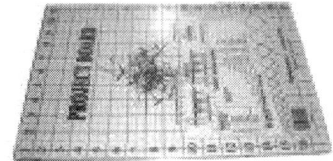

To keep the nails, you would require a Project Panel. Cardboard, clipboards, Styrofoam, and poster boards can be included.

To attach the ties to the project frame, t-nails or strong sewing nails are required, so ensure you have enough. The cross-nail method seen here is a perfect way to use nails to lock fragile ropes without reaching around the ropes.

Cellophane rolls and tape are useful and can be preserved alongside the other Macramé materials. As seen below, you should put tape on the tip of ropes to keep them from twisting.

Do you use synthetic materials, like nylon rope Parachute? If you intend to fire up the ropes, you may require a BBQ Lighter.

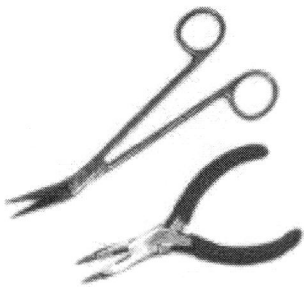

A pair of sharp scissors will be required. Fine tip longnose, tweezers, mainly if you're using beads or fine ropes, are suggested too.

For several Macramé projects, a flexible measurement tape is required.

It is easy to use fabric glue for painting and planning, so make sure to have some handy. See to it that the adhesive dries transparent.

Natural materials may require a beeswax coating, which maintains and will soften the fibers.

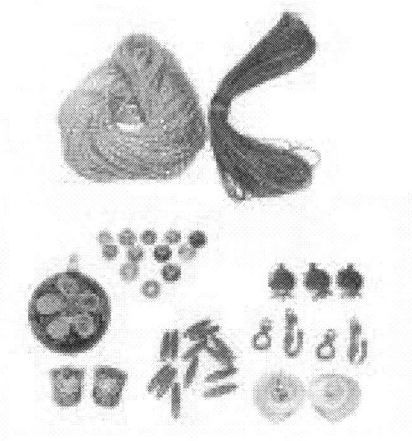

For jewelry, you would require 1 mm-2 mm string products. Beads, pendants, and clasps Micro-Macramé can also be required.

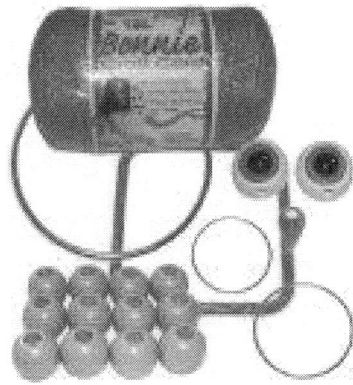

Macramé suppliers need 3 mm-6 mm rope material for regular-sized ventures.

It can often include macramé beads, circles, animal eyes, and other objects.

Difference Between A String, Rope, And Rope

Macramé String is the smooth, single twist string that Niroma Studio always began as you know it today.

String stretches faster than string or thread because it unwinds quickly such that the total width will range from 1 to 1.5 mm from when firmly wounded along the conduit to when splitting and breathable. Other retailers can mark something special, so keep that in mind.

"What's the right macramé string for beginners?" I always get questioned, and I always choose the 5 mm natural cotton string. It is the right size to hang a nice medium-sized wall, and it fits better than the 3 mm, plus it has a very compact medium twist on it, and it can be gently unknotted and reknitted a couple of times before losing its credibility as long as you are conscious. And being gentle on the hands of course always tends to keep you moving!

Macramé Rope is typically a 3-strand rope where the fibers are wrapped around each other (sometimes called a 3-ply). I saw it in four strands, but traditional rope appears to be three strands. Macramé rope is usually stronger than macramé string, and it gives you the nice, wavy fringe when you untwist it, so it's perfect for adding dimension to your job.

Since it is heavier, I like to use it for parts of items that would have to carry considerable weight. Macramé rope often stretches when it has been cut, so depending on where you stay, how much humidity you have, etc. it will also stretch up to 1 cm. Macramé Rope is typically a 6-strand (or more) braided thread, or what I believe was more widely used for macramé in the 1970s so early 1980s when the cotton string wasn't exactly 'the thing' to use. The tightly woven cotton macramé rope is sometimes called "sash rope." Sash rope is a little rigid to use and quite hard to remove, yet it's incredibly solid, so it's perfect for weight-bearing parts and if you're trying to add plenty of strength to your job. In my experience, Macramé rope is the worst on hands, but when you want a certain look or versatility, there's no discomfort, no cost!

Then there is polypropylene (or polyolefin) macramé rope, some of you may recognize one labeled variant as Bonnie Design String, which is perfect for outdoor usage because it does not shape because easily as cotton. The edge can be "frizzy," and that's only something to hold in mind.

Tools Required for Macramé

Macramé Project Board

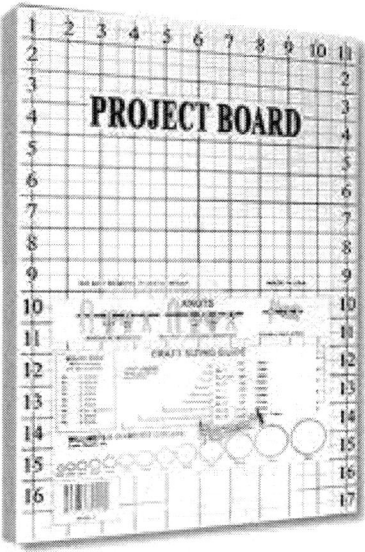

A project mounting board is a principal device required for macramé. The board is the working area where it secures the work. At art shops, you can find boards with grid inch markings and fitting directions written on the fronts. A project board may, therefore, be rendered by gluing together or using cork foam sheets. The board may be suitable for a macramé project so long as it is thick enough to prevent the nails from sticking out the back.

T-Nails

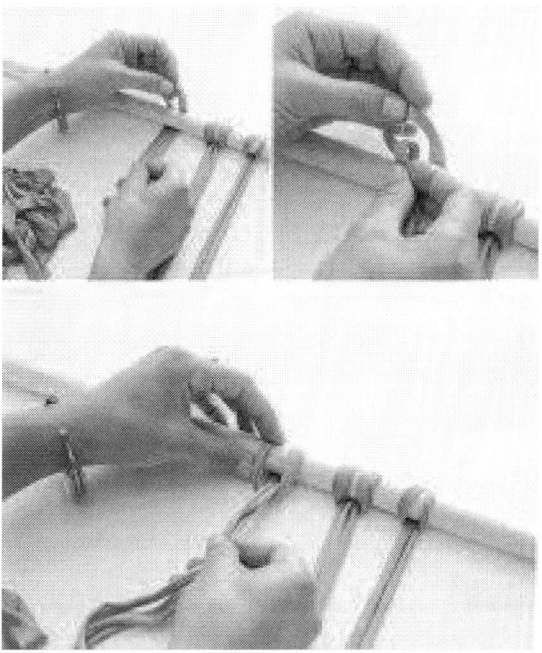

T-Nails are used to secure onto the mounting board the macramé yarn or rope. T-nails come out in various sizes. Smaller nails are ideal for smaller, more delicate designs. Nails appear to break following prolonged use. Those built of steel are more durable and can maintain for longer use.

Pattern

Many things can be created with macramé — from purses to infant mobiles. A handy tool is a macramé template. Macramé patterns provide step-by-step guidance on the knots to be used, directions for calculating, and guidelines for final assembly. Buy patterns, or you will search them online.

Scissors

A decent pair of sharp scissors could be used to cut threads correctly on a macramé layout. There are different sizes and comfort grips. Consider purchasing the sort to cover the blades with a sheath protector.

Tweezers

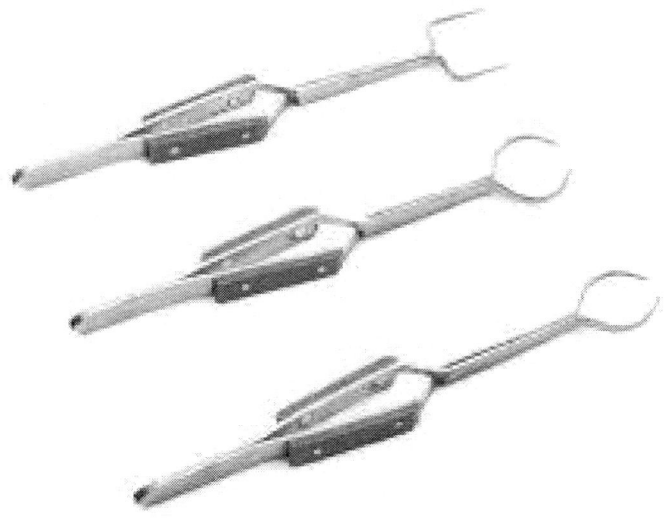

Another device used for the decoration function is tweezers. You can use a pair of tweezers to help good knot threads between the beadwork.

Needles

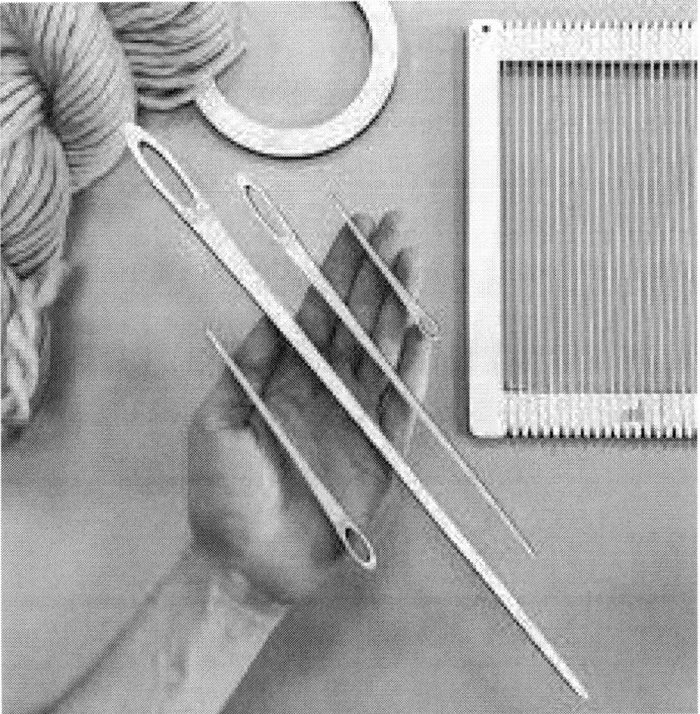

In fact, needles are used for macramé. Needles are used for the alignment of the completed product and perforation. Depending on the inclination are used blunt-end or tapestry needles and Chenille or pointed needles. Specific measurements are used to fit yarn styles like silk or nylon, and for different formed beads.

CHAPTER 5
FAQs and Things to Remember

Macrame's retro craftsmanship project has many surprising components and stunning modifications. You ought to adopt the proper strategies and procedures to practice this art or hone your talents. For an outdoor and indoor product or item, there are several ways to start a project. Here are some excellent ideas that will help to make the best of your art. However, you want.

Practice the Skill

Practice your abilities to prevent needless failures down the path before you begin to make anything. Remember, having the project going will cost you several bucks. It contains the costs you may need for equipment & accessories.

So, you can begin with a smaller practice project to improve your abilities for a bigger one instead of spending these efforts on failed attempts. It can familiarize you with numerous knots as well as designs.

Invest in The Fiber of High-Quality

The fiber's choice is by far the most important phase in the process before beginning your project. Choose the proper fiber form that may contain cords, strings, yarn, or ropes. In this range, the fiber material means the most. Cotton, cotton, jute, hemp, nylon, etc., are the options used.

For beginner-level designs, experts often consider utilizing cotton cords with just a diameter of 3 mm. To help the project, it is not only versatile & adjustable but also gentle and durable. There are also cotton ropes available in two varieties, viz—twisted and braided cords. For your project, select the thread that fits.

Maintain Sufficient Tension

You will become a specialist in the handling of a Macramé project with the necessary experience. Here the force used to strengthen the knots will mainly impact the final performance. It may even spoil other elements' consistency.

So, for consistent knotting, it makes much more sense to perform the proper amount of stress you like. If the knots in areas seem shoddy, you can need to find the appropriate combination between tightening them and loosening them.

Select Easy Patterns

Start with a basic pattern to build your masterpiece, whether working on a starter or middle-level design. It may be a plain square knot or a square knot that alternates.

There are simple, easy ways to-make patterns. In these models, you will learn to maintain uniformity. It would be best if you also used the independent boards or anchoring strategies to hold the work-in-progress stable in place.

Using the Right Rope Amount

The number of ropes you require is 5-6 times the completed item's total length. Still hold the tip of an additional cord length at the bottom of the thing to create fringes and other decorative accents. You do not want a short rope, as it will thoroughly spoil your project.

Even attaching ropes, later on, is tough. Around the same moment, though, there's still no reason to waste the remaining strings. You may do smaller projects for the shorter cords, such as jewelry, bookmarks, or key chains.

FAQs

Can Macrame Be Washed?

YES. Macrame is very stable and does not readily fall apart. In a tiny garment bag, it can be a machine, washed at 86°F. Only hang to dry.

Can You Use Yarn to Macrame?

YES. It's possible to use yarn. You can realize that only the scale of macramé knots would be as wide as the thread or substance you are using. The smaller your choice of string, yarn, or cord, the smaller the knots would be. The loops would not be very clear if the thread is too thin. Instead of a bigger project like the wall hanging, yarn may be perfectly adjusted to the micro-macrame project to be used in jewelry making, for example.

Can You Macrame With Jute?

YES. Macrame artists used jute and hemp popularly, but the lack of consumer demand led to nylon and the satin rayon macrame cords, and other human-made fibers. Nylon cords or cotton are preferred for beginners because, in the event of an error, they are simple to unravel.

How to Choose What Sort of Macrame Cord to Utilized for Our Project?

When choosing your content, there are several things to consider. There's always something apparent to consider availability and cost. But with your idea, you will also want to understand the strength of the content. For example, if you want to hang a vine, you want to use a stronger rope, such as those made of jute, ribbon, leather, nylon, or cotton.

Furthermore, you should consider a cord's stiffness. You would want to use shorter, more lightweight cords for jewelry, such as a cotton embroidery cord that is very smooth and flexible. When creating an outdoor project, you may want to use a sturdy and long-lasting polypropylene chain, either the outdoor plant keeper or an outdoor hammock.

What Size Cord Should We Use?

You would want to select the thickness of 4.0 mm or more for the larger decorations like the wall hangings or the plant holders, depending on the project. You can use a cord shorter than 2.0 mm in diameter for the smaller micro-macrame designs, such as bracelets and necklaces.

How Much Cord Do We Need for Macrame?

The cords you will use for knotting would need to be between 5 to 6 times the length of the completed one. The cords that are your "core" cords used for the form but that is not necessarily knotted may just need to be around twice the final length. For having a fringe or the other decorative attachments at the ends, note to leave additional cord length. And rather than too little, it's better to have much rope. At the top, you can still trim lengthy bits.

How Do We Keep Our Knots Looking Uniform?

The easiest way to ensure that the knots are uniform, to make certain that the friction on your cords is kept equally and that every knot lines up straight, vertically, horizontally, and diagonally on both sides. You would want to check and knot, particularly when you are only learning, confirm that its lines with the proceeding knot edges are strong and that the loops are even. The only way to make sure that the project is successful is to protect the project. You'll like to hang them from the clothes rack or a safe hook for larger ventures. Ideally, you can hang from two points on the project so that the project does not rock back and forth. You'll like to make a macrame board for the smaller projects like the jewelry.

What Is the Macrame Board?

The macrame board is a location where you protect your knitting project. This can be created from several different materials, but you essentially want to make a firm surface where you can insert pins. A corkboard, a sheet of polyurethane, or the two pieces of the cardboard bound together may be used. Without poking out the other side, the board should be around 12 inches square and thick to put a T pin or the corsage pin in.

Why Is Macrame Getting Back?

Macrame was popular with the hippie movement back in the 1970s, but as a part of the latest tribal and the Boho (Bohemian) style trends in the home decor, it has moved back into fashion.

Where Did Macrame Originate?

Macrame is believed to derive from the Arabic term migramah, meaning fringe, which corresponds to the custom of the 13th century used by Arab weavers for creating decorating the fringes on the camels and the horses to keep animals safe from the flies. It can also come from a Turkish word for napkin or towel, meaning "makrama." Macrame was used as a means to protect the loomed fabrics' lower edges. Macrame's first known uses occurred in Babylonians and Assyrians' decorative carvings. Macrame was most common in the Victorian period, where most homes were decorated with this art in products such as bedspreads, tablecloths, and curtains. Queen Mary also taught her ladies-in-waiting Macrame in the 17th century. In the 19th century, Macrame was also a favorite pastime of the British and the American sailors who made tiny crafts that they either sold or exchanged in port.

Additional Macrame Resources

- Free Macrame Patterns – For additional Macrame results, this is a great website. They have papers for beginners, a dictionary of words widely used, and a children's section. They also offer several free patterns of Macrame. A variety of macrame pattern books, decorative macrame beads & dyed macrame cord, and rings are available in their Etsy store.

- Modern Macrame– This website has a wealth of macrame data and tools, including a selection of dyed macrame cords and handy DIY Macrame kits and designs. They provide the Kit of Macrame Wall Hanging for $36 and the Macrame Plant Hanger Kits for $36, which contains everything that you need to finish your first basic macrame project, for a really simple way to start. They also have a book by Emily Katz, "Modern Macrame: that contains 33 Stylish Projects for the Handmade Home," which has some lovely projects that you would enjoy.

- Pepperell Braiding Company– It is another outstanding website for macrame cords and accessories. Decorative items such as beads and supplies such as wooden dowels are also sold, plus a range of cords and DIY kits.

CHAPTER 6
Macrame Easy and Fun Project 1

Hoop Earrings

If you fancy trying your hand at the art of macramé jewelry, this project is a great place to begin. A pair of shop-bought hoop earrings are covered with an easy square knot pattern, embellished with round metallic beads. They are so simple-to-making that you'll want to create several pairs in a variety of colors to complement your fashion choices.

MATERIALS:

- 2.6m (9ft) length of 1mm (1/32in) nylon bead cord in a color of your choice
- Pair of 4cm (11/2in) hoop earrings
- Six 4mm (5/32in) round metallic beads with a 2mm (3/32in) hole

KNOTS & TECHNIQUES:

- Square Knot
- Overhand Knot

PREPARATION:

- Cut two 1.3m (41/2ft) lengths of 1mm (1/32in) nylon bead cord

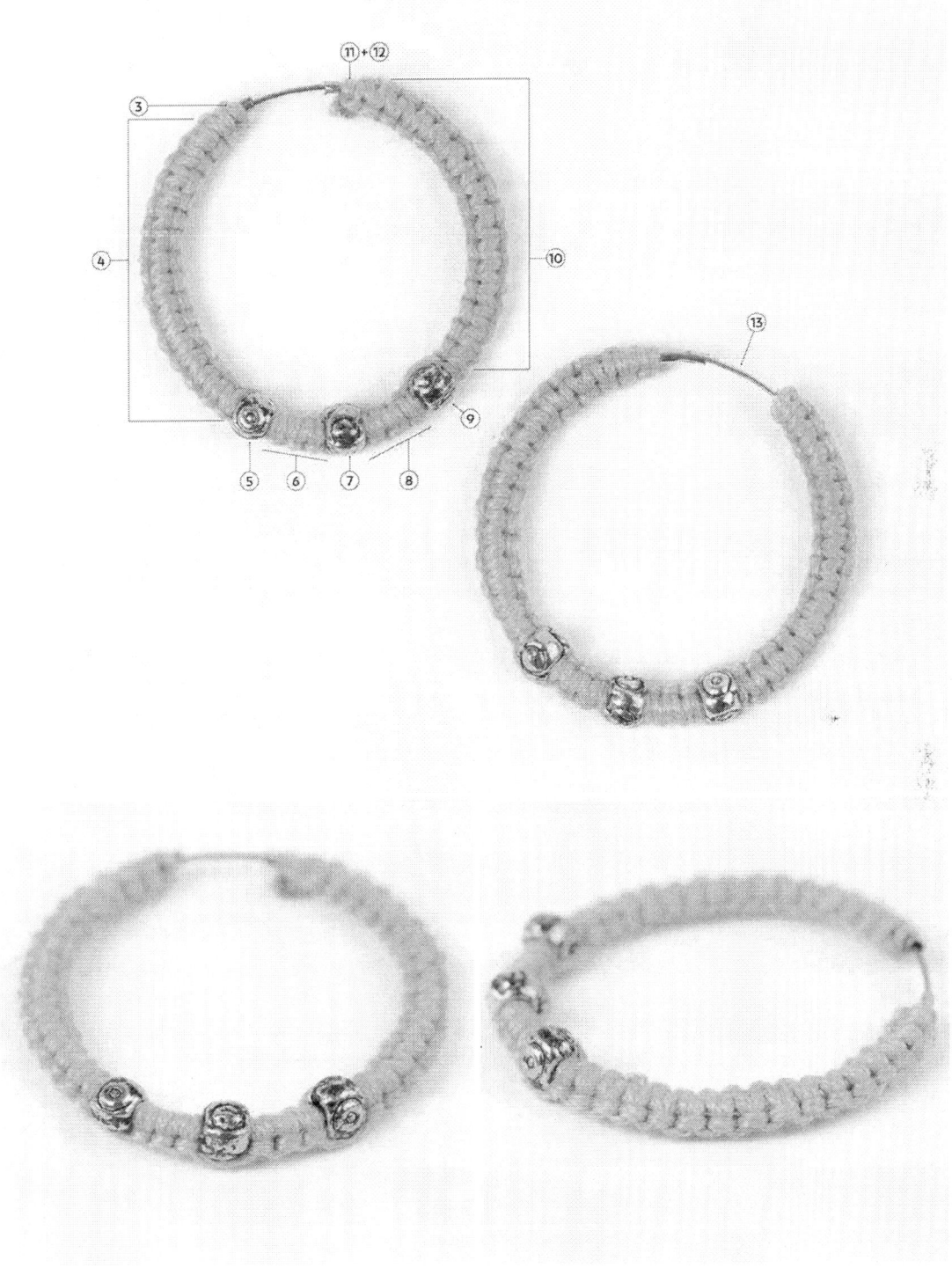

Method

1. Fold one of the 1.3m (41/2ft) lengths of nylon bead cord in half over the inside of one of the hoop earrings.

2. Secure the hoop earring to a project board using T-pins. The hoop will be used as your filler cord and each side of the folded cord as your working cords.

3. Tie a firm square knot as close as possible to where the connector inserts into the hoop.

4. Tie a sinnet of fifteen square knots working your way around the hoop (your filler cord). Push the knots firmly together once the sinnet is complete.

5. Thread a metal bead onto the earring hoop and push it firmly against the square knot sinnet.

6. Directly beneath the bead, tie a sinnet of three-square knots.

7. Repeat step 5.

8. Repeat step 6.

9. Repeat step 5.

10. Directly beneath the bead, tie a sinnet of sixteen square knots to finish just before the connector.

11. Tie a tight double overhand knot with both cords.

12. Trim the cords and carefully singe the ends to prevent fraying. Use a flame to melt the cord ends but be sure to stop before they char.

13. Repeat steps 1–12 with the second hoop earring to complete the pair.

Choker Necklace

The delicate 'links of this exquisite choker-style necklace are created using square knots embellished with metallic beads, and the finished piece is secured in place around your neck with plaited ties. Simply adjust the length of the plaits to make the necklace longer or shorter to fit. You can make a bracelet or an anklet to match your choker necklace – just tie fewer 'links'.

MATERIALS:

- 12m (40ft) length of 1mm (1/32in) nylon bead cord in a color of your choice
- 8mm (5/16in) jump ring
- Fourteen 4mm (5/32in) round metallic beads with 2mm (3/32in) hole

KNOTS & TECHNIQUES:

- Reverse Lark's Head Knot
- Square Knot
- Overhand Knot
- Numbering Cords
- Plaiting

PREPARATION:

- Cut eight 150cm (5ft) lengths of 1mm (1/_32_in) nylon bead cord

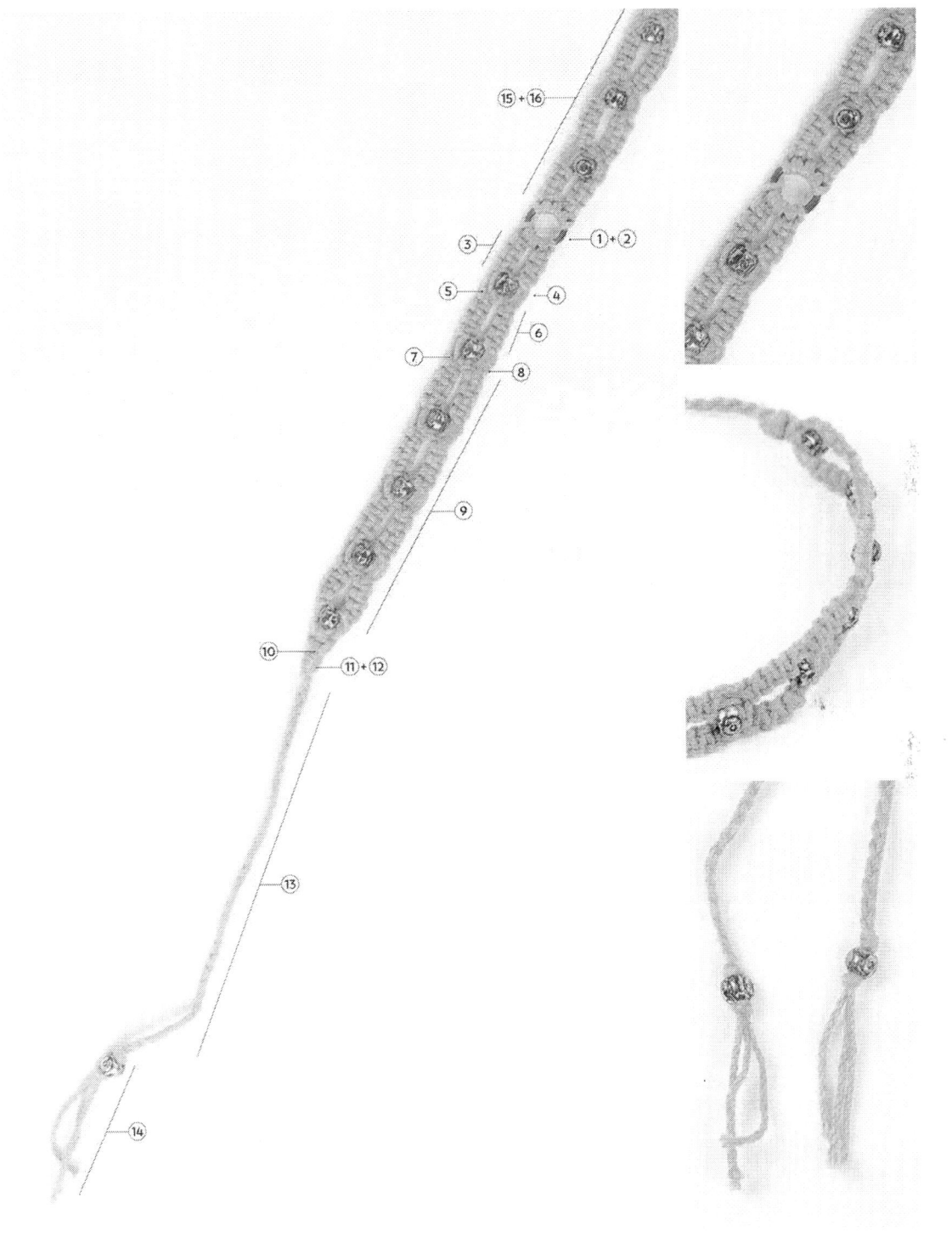

Method

1. Secure the jump ring to the top of a project board using a T-pin.

2. Mount four 150cm (5ft) lengths of nylon bead cord onto the jump ring with reverse lark's head knots.

3. Separate the cords into two groups of four cords and tie a sinnet of three-square knots with each group.

4. Number the cords 1 to 8. Thread a metal bead onto cords 4 and 5 so that the bead sits directly against the square knots above it.

5. Tie a square knot directly beneath the metal bead using cords 4 and 5 as filler cords and cords 3 and 6 as working cords.

6. Separate the cords into two groups of four cords and tie a sinnet of four-square knots with each group.

7. Number the cords 1 to 8. Thread a metal bead onto cords 4 and 5 so that it sits directly against the square knots above it.

8. Tie a square knot directly beneath your metal bead using cords 4 and 5 as filler cords and cords 3 and 6 as working cords.

9. Repeat steps 6–8 four more times.

10. Number the cords 1 to 8. Tie an 8-cord square knot using cords 3– 6 as filler cords and cords 1 and 2 and 7 and 8 as working cords.

11. Directly beneath the 8-cord square knot, tie an overhand knot using all eight cords and pull really tightly to secure.

12. Cut off five of the cords just beneath the overhand knot and carefully singe the ends with a flame to melt them, taking care not to char them, then press them onto the knot.

13. With the remaining three cords, make a 12cm (43/4in) plait and tie a tight overhand knot to secure.

14. Thread a metal bead onto the cords and secure with a tight overhand knot, then trim the cords to your desired length.

15. Unpin the half-completed necklace from the project board, rotate it through 180 degrees and reattach the jump ring to the top of the project board (the completed half of the choker is still right side facing up but it is now trailing off of the top of the project board).

16. Now repeat steps 2–14 on the other side of the jump ring to complete the necklace.

Hanging Light

Made with a simple yet effective half knot spiral pattern, this hanging light is a great macramé starter project – it's an easy DIY undertaking that enables you to create something special for your home. To create something really awe inspiring, you could make multiple lights and hang them in conjunction with each other for your very own installation piece.

MATERIALS:

- 27m (89ft) length of 8mm (5/16in) rope
- 90cm (3ft) length of 4mm (5/32in) twisted rope
- 3m (10ft) DIY fabric cord set with plug, lead and E27 lamp holder

KNOTS & TECHNIQUES:

- Half Knot Spiral
- Wrapped Knot

PREPARATION:

- Firmly secure the lamp holder to a horizontal rail around 2m (61/2ft) high so that the electrical cord hangs down vertically

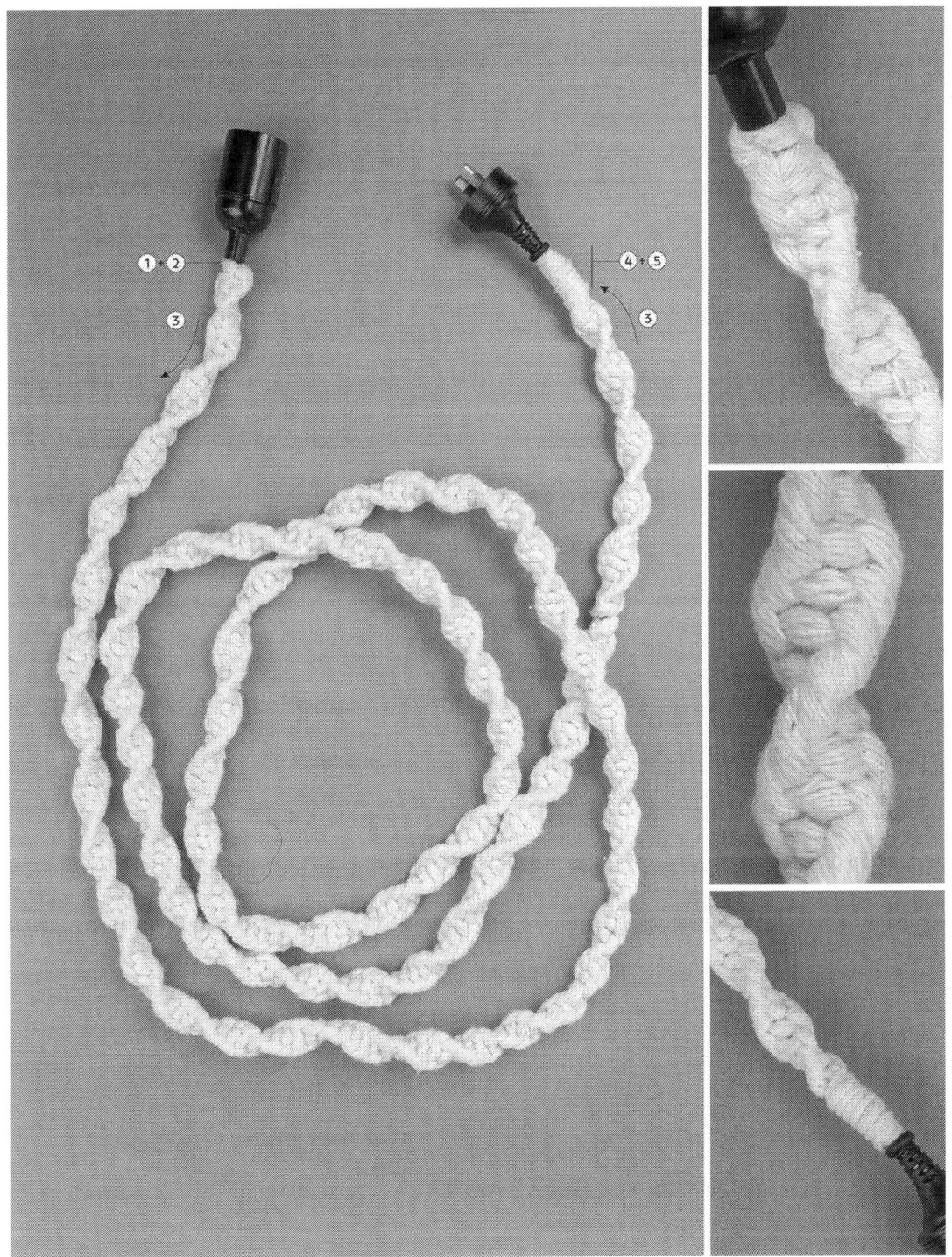

Method

1. Fold the 27m (89ft) length of 8mm (5/16in) rope in half and place the halfway point behind the electrical cord and as close to the lamp holder as possible.

2. Begin to tie a half knot spiral using the electrical cord as the filler cord and the rope as the working cords, making sure to push your first half knot firmly against the lamp holder.

3. Continue to tie a half knot spiral until you are 3cm (11/8in) from the plug.

4. Trim the excess rope just above the plug and push the ends down flat against the electrical cord.

5. Using the 90cm (3ft) length of 4mm (5/32in) twisted rope, tie a wrapped knot starting directly under your last half knot and over the rope ends to finish directly above the plug so that all the electrical cord is covered.

Pendant Lantern

The shape of this beautiful decoration has been inspired by the open latticework of Moroccan lanterns and it will provide you with a beautiful feature anywhere in your home. It could be styled as a mobile in a baby's nursery or to hang as a decorative piece alongside your hanging planters.

MATERIALS:

- 106m (351ft) length of 5mm (1/4in) rope
- 2.5cm (1in) metal ring
- Cane rings: one 10cm (4in); one 13cm (5in); two 20cm (8in)

KNOTS & TECHNIQUES:

- Double Half Hitch
- Reverse Lark's Head Knot
- Square Knot
- Triple Half Hitch

PREPARATION:

- Cut twenty-four 4m (131/4ft) lengths of 5mm (1/4in) rope

- Cut two 5m (161/2ft) lengths of 5mm (1/4in) rope

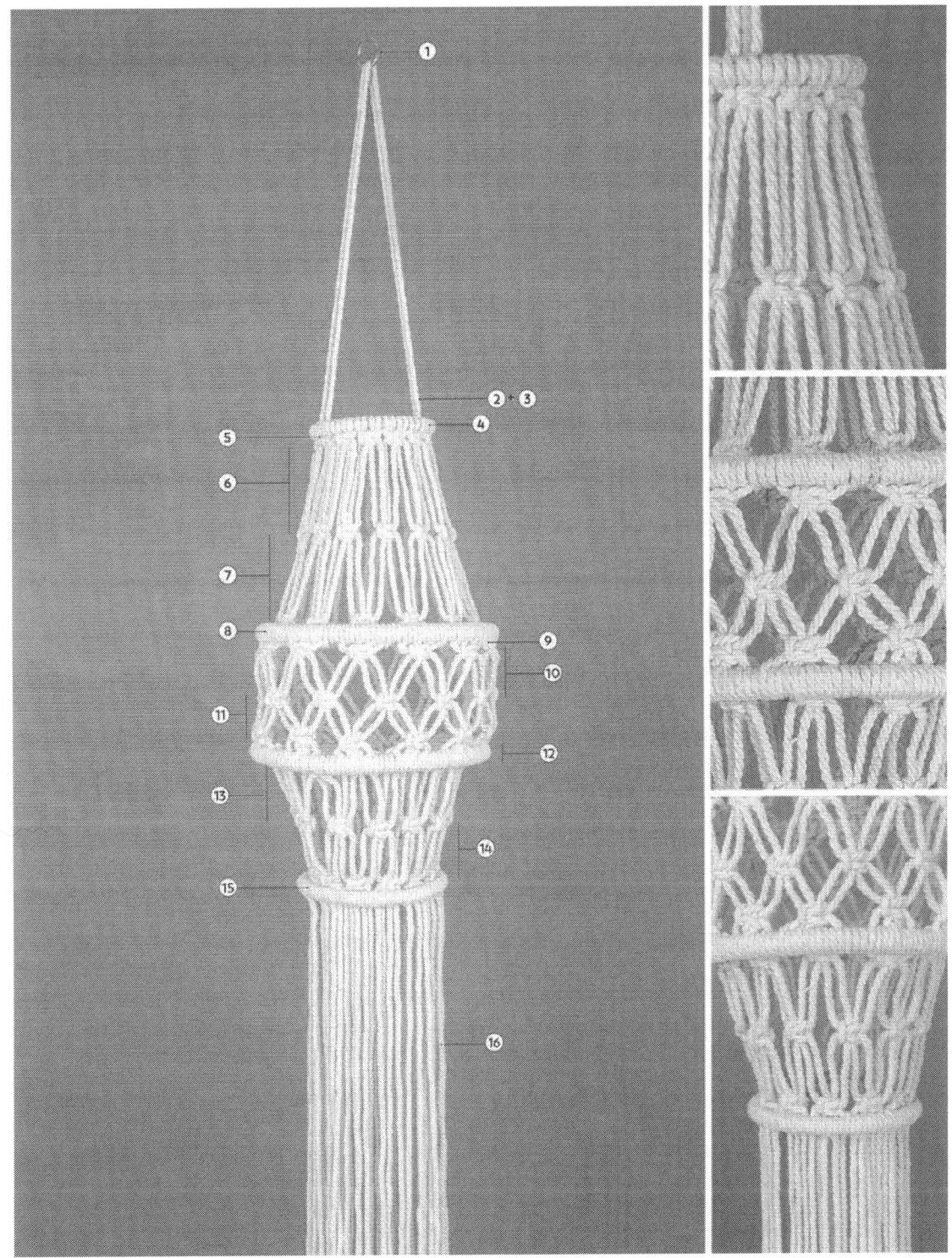

Method

1. Take both of the 5m (161/2ft) lengths of rope and fold them in half over the inside of the metal ring to give you four equal lengths of rope hanging down.

2. Place all four cords inside the 10cm (4in) cane ring. The cane ring sitting horizontally is now to be used as the holding cord.

3. Take two adjacent cords, drop down 30cm (12in) and tie the cords onto the ring with double half hitches. Repeat to tie the remaining two cords onto the opposite side of the cane ring.

4. Attach twenty-four of the 4m (131/4ft) lengths of rope to the cane ring – twelve cords to each half – using reverse lark's head knot.

5. Secure the cords to the ring by tying a row of thirteen square knots directly beneath the cane ring.

6. Alternate cords, drop down 7cm (23/4in) and tie a row of thirteen square knots.

7. Alternate cords, drop down 7cm (23/4in) and tie another row of thirteen square knots.

8. Place all cords inside one of the 20cm (8in) cane rings. This cane ring sitting horizontally is now to be used as the holding cord. Tie all cords onto the cane ring using triple half hitches.

9. Secure the cords to the cane ring by tying a row of thirteen square knots directly beneath.

10. Alternate cords, drop down 3cm (11/8in) and tie a row of thirteen square knots.

11. Alternate cords, drop down 3cm (11/8in) and tie another row of thirteen square knots.

12. Repeat steps 8 and 9 with the second 20cm (8in) cane ring.

13. Alternate cords, drop down 4.5cm (13/4in) and tie a row of thirteen square knots.

14. Alternate cords, drop down 4.5cm (13/4in) and tie another row of thirteen square knots.

15. Place all cords inside the 13cm (5in) cane ring. This cane ring sitting horizontally is now to be used as the holding cord. Tie all cords onto the cane ring using double half hitches.

16. Trim the cords to 65cm (251/2in) or to your desired length.

CHAPTER 7
Macrame Easy and Fun Project 2

Macrame Curtain

Things you'll need:

- Rope
- Window rod/Wood dowel
- Masking tape
- Scissor

Steps

1. On a foam core frame, bind four strands together and insert pins into the top knot and the two middle strands at the bottom to hold those in place.

2. Take a right outer string (pink) and move it over the other two middle strands on the left side. Take a left (yellow) outer strand and move it under the pink string, behind the central strand, and on the other hand, over the pink strand.

3. Pull firmly on the two fibers. Now, during the first step, you revert to what you did! End up taking the outer edge left string (which has become the pink one) and lay two strands in the center. Take a right outermost strand (which is now the yellow one) and move under the pink one, behind the two middle strings, and on the other hand, over the pink one. Drag these two strands close until they create a knot from the preceding stage with the twisted strands. The toughest thing is that! These simple movements only replicate the rest of the actions.

4. Using four additional strands, repeat directions 1-3 to create another knot straight next to the first knot. To create a new community with the two leftmost strings of the second knot, carry the two rightmost strings of the first knot.

5. For the new group, repeat the fundamental knot by trying to take the external right strand (purple) and moving it over the central two strands on the left side's Take the outer left (green) strand and move it under the purple string, behind the central strand, and on the other hand, over the purple strand.

6. Pull firmly on the two fibers. Invert the first move now! End up taking the outer left string (now the purple one) and lay two strands in the center. Take a right outermost strand (that is now the green one) and move it under the purple one, above the middle two strands, and on the other side, over the purple one. Tightly pull the two strands.

7. Split the middle group of threads by shifting the two leftmost strings left and the two rightmost threads right. For both groups, repeat the simple knot and start this method until you've completed as many rows as you like.

8. You will see that the idea of creating the simple knots with the yarn in the steps seems to be the same, but just on a far larger scale.

9. Hang your fresh curtain in the perfect position until you stop braiding the cords. To finish, tie masking tape across the ends just before the rope meets the floor Break the tape into it, leaving 2/3 or half of the tape on the string untouched. This would hopefully prevent the ends from creasing overtime.

DIY Macrame Yarn Garland

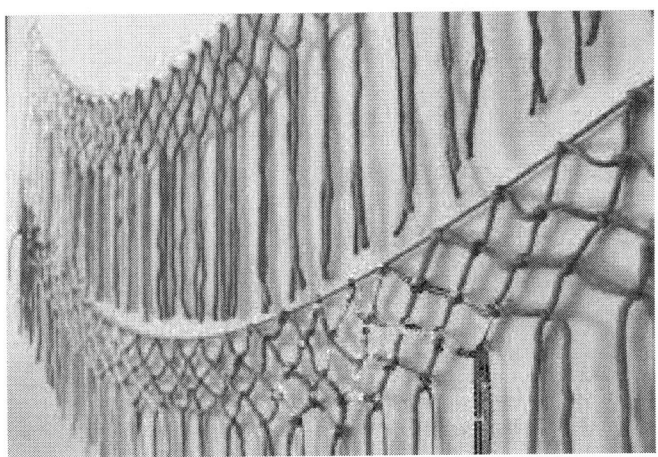

Things you'll need:

- Chunky yarn (Assorted colors)
- washi tape or push pins
- Scissors

Steps

1. For your framework, cut one length of yarn as long as you want. Then, based on how much fringe you choose to hang down, cut up pieces of yarn that are about 2' long. You can still cut these up to be still later, but they'll get shorter when you tie them together. To complement this size garland, you can need just around 30-35 separate cuts of yarn.

2. With push pins, hang the framework strand on the wall and then insert the individual pieces by attaching a single knot around the framework. Tie the first-knot row

3. Then, by dropping the first yarn strand and binding a double knot with the second and third strings, begin the second row of knots.

4. Then begin binding the next two strands of yarn about 2 "down together, making sure they were more balanced on the base piece of yarn between the knots.

5. Then continue back where the second row of knots began but attach a knot with the first and second strands. And proceed to tie knots about 2 "below the last knot all the way through. Once the second row was finished, let it go back on its left side again. The first strand was set alone, and the second and third strands were knotted again, and the process repeated all the way around.

6. Your last move is to cut the edges to make them equal, and you're done.

Macrame Trim Fring Pillow Cover

Things you'll need:

- In the proportions of your pillow insert, a simple linen zipper pillow cover

- An array of fringe-y decorative trim

- Yard Stick

- Scissors

- Fabric Pen Washable

- Fabric Glue (Liquid Stitch used)

- Fray Check

Steps

1. Layout the cover for the plain pillow.

2. The first row of fringe trim is being cut to be the same width as the pillowcase. No need for measurements! Only line them up, cut them!

3. Layout and cut the remaining of your trim rows to length, and spend a little time modifying them before you have them on the final product exactly as you like them.

4. Make little outlines on the sides of where your glue line is going to be, so you can utilize your yardstick (or something with a straight edge) to link the dots and create a straight line with your fabric marking pen as you eliminate the fringe trim.

5. On your fabric glue, make sure to fulfill all the directions to stretch out an even strip of glue upon one of the pen lines. Then starting at one end and push down the fringe trim carefully as you move. It's cool if it doesn't go down smoothly, so before the glue dries, you have some time to acclimate.

6. Remember! You may use a sewing machine rather than fabric glue for this, so you don't want to bother about having to bend the pillow cover so that it doesn't sew on all layers.

7. Stand back to ensure that it's even and smooth, tweaking if required. Then glue the rest of the rows in the same direction!

8. Repeat these moves until they match each other on the opposite side of the cover. And use the Fray Test on the edges to avoid fraying on your trim.

9. To personalize a pillow cover, use the Macramé Fringe Trim.

Macrame Feather

Things you'll need:

- 5 mm Cotton Single tie String

- Cloth stiffener

- Fabric scissors must be sharp

- Cat Brush

- Ruler

For a feather of medium size, cut:

For the spine, 1 32-inch strand

For the top, 10-12 14-inch strands

For middle, 8-10 12-inch strands

For bottom, 6-8 10-inch strands

Fold in half the 32 "strand. consider taking one of the 14" threads, fold it in half, and under the spine squish it.

75

Steps

1. Take another 14-inch thread, fold it in half, and put it into the top horizontal string loop. Drag it across and lay it on top of the opposite strand horizontally.

2. Now, via the top string, draw the lower strings all the way. This is your knot.

3. Tightly pull both ends. You'll rotate the start side to the next row. So, if you first lay the horizontal thread from left to right, you'll lay the next horizontal thread from right to left.

4. Lay under the spine the first folded strand, thread another tucked strand into its loop. Drag the top loop through the lower strands. And tighten.

5. Keep on working and operate down in size steadily.

6. Move the threads up to tighten-catch the edge of the middle (spine) string with one hand and move the strands up with another. Pull the fringe back to reach the edge of the middle strand until you're finished.

7. Consider giving it a rough trim, then. This not only serves to direct the design but also serves to smooth the strands out. To be realistic, the smaller the strands, the smoother. It also helps to get a very sharp set of fabric shears! Place the feather on a sturdy surface after a coarse trim, as you will need a pet brush to brush off the cording. The brush can harm any fragile or wood surface, so consider using a cutting mat for self-healing or even a scorched cardboard box. Begin at the spine when brushing and move deep into the cord while brushing. To get the perfect, soft fringe, it'll take many deep strokes.

8. Work your way downward. Keep the lower part of the spine as brushing while you're at the edge-you don't want the comb to yank some strands off!

9. Next, the feather will be stiffened. The cording is so delicate that if you scoop it up and attempt to hang it, it will only flop. Give it a spray or two, then take a couple of hours to try. You may now go back to add a final trim after the feather has stiffened up somewhat. This is the most critical aspect. Make it easy. It's safer to trim fewer than more! Depending on how much you move the piece, you will need to adjust the trim. After you're finished trimming, for good measure, you may also send it another slip of fabric stiffener. And then, you'll be prepared.

Simple Dip Dyed Macrame Wall Hanging

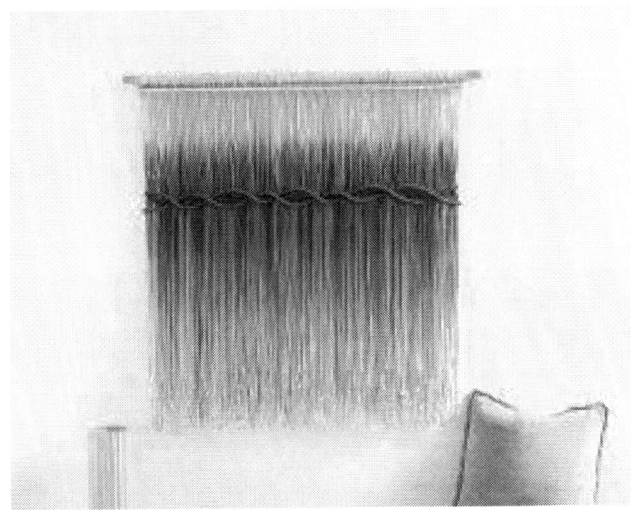

Things you'll need:

- 3 mm macramé thread of Cotton
- 12" rod of wooden dowel
- Scissors
- Liquid Dye for Fabric
- Plastic or Container of Metal
- Gloves
- Salt
- Liquid Soap

Steps

1. Consider cutting an even amount of 3-meter-long cord lengths.
2. Next, use a lark head knot to tie each string to the dowel. Wrap the string in half to do this, but the tucked end across and at the back of the dowel, and draw the tails via the string, eventually.

3. Attach lark head knot cords for macramé wall hanging. Using this method, tie all of the strings to the dowel rod.

4. Only one kind of macramé knot, the square knot, is used to create the remainder of this wall hanging.

5. You want four strands to create a square knot. In order to secure the knot along the two central strings, the two outer strands would be used.

6. Over the 2 middle strings, traverse the left-hand string.

7. On top of the left-hand string, beneath the two middle strings,

8. move the right-hand string and up via the loop created by the left thread. To strengthen pull.

9. On the other side, reverse this process: across the two central strands, jump the right-hand string.

10. Move the left-hand string, under the 2 central strings, over the right-hand string, and up thru the loop created by the right thread. To strengthen pull.

11. End up making square knots all the way around the rod for the first row.

12. For the 2nd row, from two consecutive square knots, you can create the square knots utilizing two strands, respectively. Now, for this section, the strands which were center strings in the preceding row would be outside strands. In the final step, swapping rows to give you a cool mesh design.

13. Create a knot allying each of the prior row's square knots. Two strands on either hand would not be used with this second row of knots.

14. For row 3, you again render square knots (a total of 9 knots) between the knots of the prior row. In this section, the strings on the ends that were not included in the prior row will be included again.

15. In this design, begin creating knots until your section is as broad as you'd like it to be.

16. Eventually, to cut up and balance out the fringe, use scissors. Like I did, you can trim the tails equally or go for a level, stages, or a more natural presentation.

17. If you want to preserve the piece in its organic cotton color, then at this stage, you're done. Let's whip out the hue and add a burst of color.

18. Fill a tub of warm water first.

19. Next, spill in the liquid coloring agent,

20. Before putting it in the dye tub, get the macramé wet.

21. And, in the dye tub, add it. For around ten minutes, begin by bringing only the bottom half or so in and then shift a little further down for the next five or so mins. Finally, to have the softest color at the end, I only sunk the last few inches in slightly.

22. Finally, underneath running cold water, drain the dyed item unless it remains clear.

23. And that is that! When your hanging macramé wall has dried, it's all set to hang.

CHAPTER 8
Macrame Easy and Fun Project 3

Chic DIY Plant Hanger

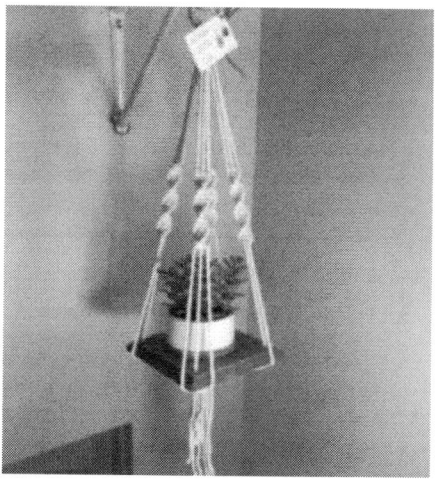

Materials

- 3 nice, strong, and colorful cords
- Scissors
- 6 wooden beads
- A ring
- A plant vase

Instructions

1. Pass two cords out of the three through the ring, leaving it to go without any pattern for a reasonable distance. Insert three beads and knot with a double half-hitch knotting method.

2. Insert the beads on the other side and make the same double half-hitch knot.

3. Take one cord from each one of the two sides and entwine them using the same knotting pattern.

4. Do this on the other side too.

5. Now leave about three inches and knot the cords again.

6. Put the plant vase in place. Take the remaining cord and tie the four cords neatly and carefully.

7. Leave the strands to go down the length of your choice and cut off the extra strands.

8. Your chic macramé DIY plant hanger is ready to be hanged!

Macramé in an Aluminum Chair

I have a tough time saying no to antique aluminum seats. They are such a symbol for the summer and can come in some fantastic colors. Unfortunately, some of them had too much use, and the webbing had become fragile and thread able. I was not sure if one of them was going to survive another summer, so I wanted to see if I could give it new life. Macramé seemed to be one of the few choices, but I did not know if I wanted to bother with all the knot-tying, and I was on a late weaving trip, so I loved the knots and settled on vintage-inspired colors on a beautiful geometric pattern.

Materials

- Chair with aluminum (mine is child-sized)
- Paracord and macramé cord in different colors but identical in scale (150'-200' overall, depending on the height of the chair)
- Scarves
- Screwdriver on flathead
- Rubber belt

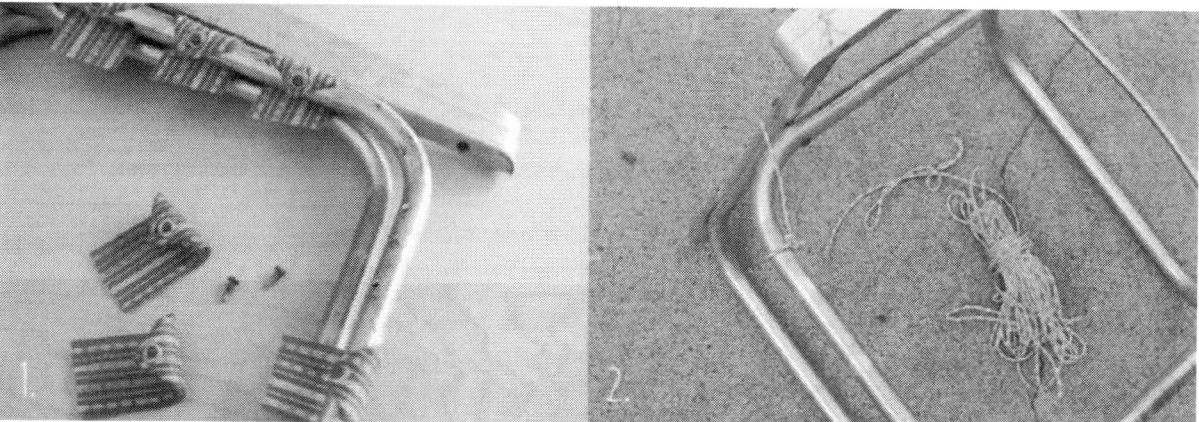

Step 1: Strip webbing from your chair by removing the ties and unwinding the posts on the back of your frame.

Step 2: Determine which color you want to start with and tie a double knot at the edge of the flat front, around the frame cover. Leave only five inches of the tail. I used a rubber band to tie my paracord and macramé cord loosely together, as I twisted it to prevent it from being tangled too far.

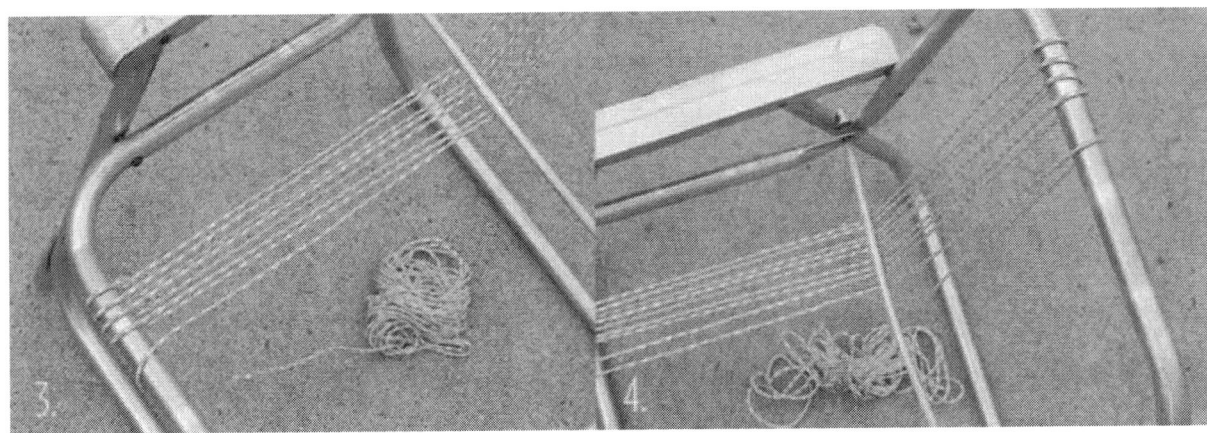

Step 3: Loop the rope at the turn of the chair under the central bar, and up and over the top of the frame. Then curl back under the curve of the chair, and coil around the seat frame's bottom edge, next to where you started.

Step 4: All your rows will extend from the front to the back of the edges of the frame. Continue to switch colors or run out of thread. Bind a double knot around either the top or bottom side of the frame depending on where you end up. Make sure you are left with enough cord to tuck in when you are finished. As seen below, you can tie into the next color or cord string too.

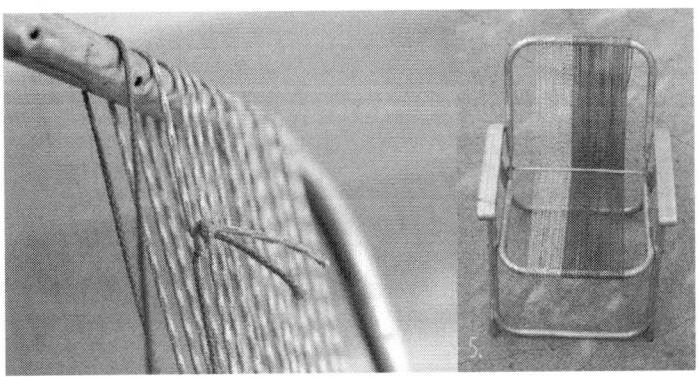

Step 5: Loop until the other end of the flat portion of the frame is passed to you. The rounded corner will have a slight negative space, but do not worry. That should be the way it should be.

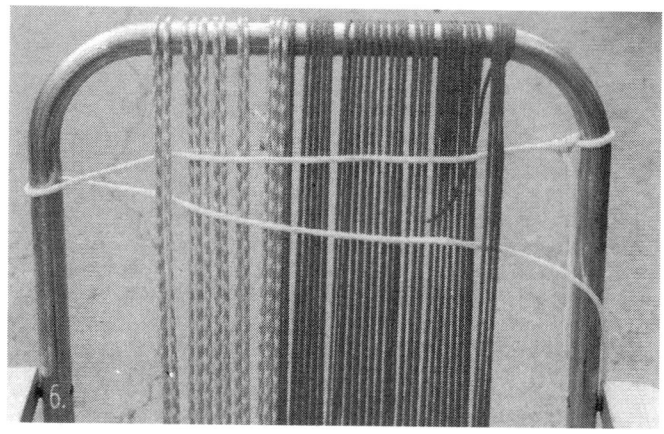

Step 6: Only tie the side of the frame with a double knot, to continue weaving in the other direction, and leave around 5 inches of the tail. Take your cord under the first four rows and make the triangle shape (two top and two bottoms to get four total), then come up and over with your thread. Tuck it under; you have got four more on the other end. On the other hand, loop the rope over the top of the frame, and go back the same way you came in, as shown above.

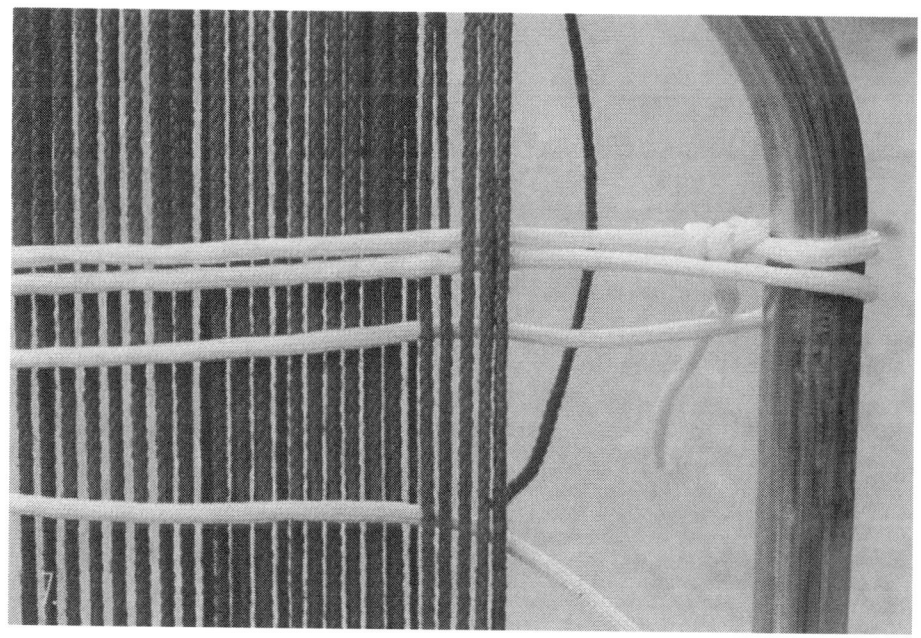

Step 7: Wrap around the frame's starting side and come up under that first four and the next two, so you are skipping a total of six cords. Only replicate that same amount on the opposite side, and then return the way you came in.

Stage 8: Keep repeating this method of can two rows each time you cross, and then proceed back the same way you came along, creating a triangular pattern. Keep with that cord, before you stop or have to tie to another end of the same color.

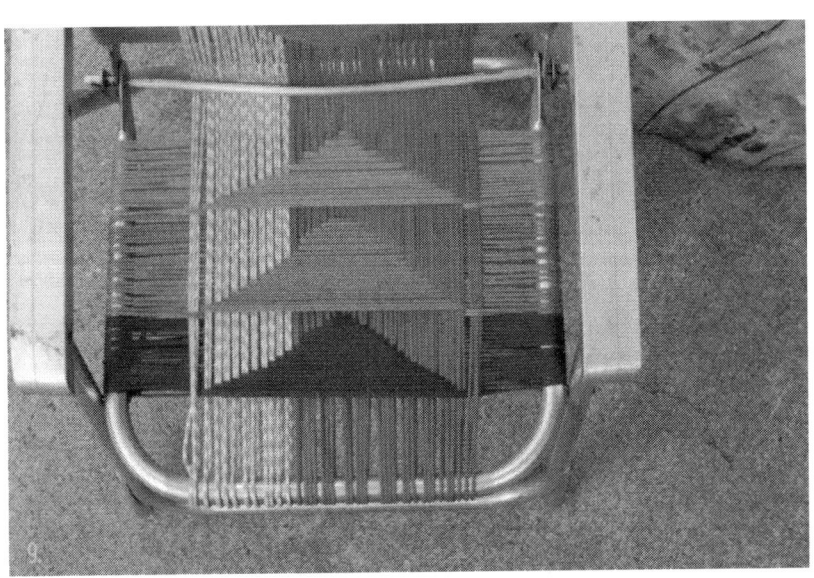

Stage 9: This is what a new triangle looks like to turn colors. For this size of the frame, I ended up with three on the bottom and three on the top. If you are using an adult chair, I would recommend that you use a thicker macramé cord to make work easier.

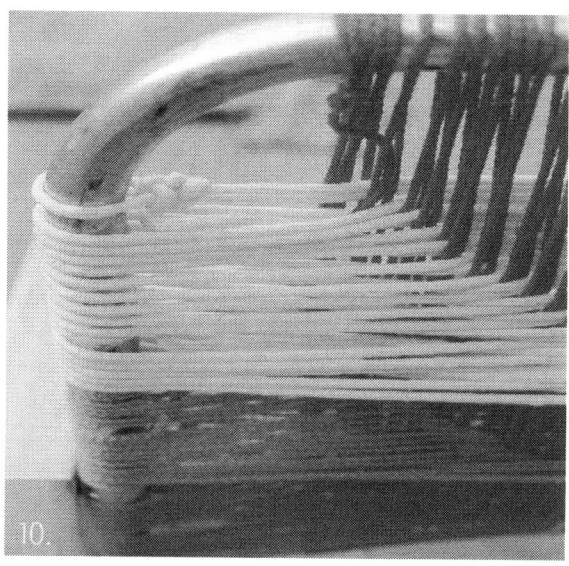

Stage 10: Trim the loose tails, so they are long enough to tuck in and relax in. If this were a macramé project, it would be better to hide the loose ends, but we are just spinning and putting the fancy knot-tying onto another job.

This was one of the most time-consuming projects I have been doing lately, so it might be a while before I can complete another, but after Sebastian saw this one, he placed an order for a red, white, and blue chair with a big 'X' on the top and bottom. We shall see.

I learned a lot about this project by trial and error. If you tug too hard on the first round of woven sheets, you will end up with a chair that will not remain open after a second sheet has been woven even tighter.

Sometimes, if you get your rows too close to the rounded edges, they roll over and mess up your pattern in a perfectly spaced way.

Toilet Paper Holders

Materials

- 11 cords of 13 inches each

- Scissors

- Tape measure

- Macramé board

Instructions

1. Get nine cords, divide it into three, to have three cords on each side; braid the cords together.

2. Get one cord from the two remaining ones: place it at one end of the braid. Make a loop with it, and carefully and neatly tie it to that end, so it will have an aesthetic look.

3. Do the same with the other cord at the other end, and you will have a new holder for your tissue paper. Not just any holder, but a macramé holder!

Macramé Bathmat

Materials

- 3 bundles of strong and hard cords, as the texture of jute
- Scissors
- Matching color of thread and needle
- A macramé boards.

Instructions

1. With the three bundles of cords, form a tight loop.
2. From the loop, make the second, third, and fourth loop.
3. Continue looping and get the rope to be as long as possible. Make enough loops that will suffice for the whole mat.
4. When any one of the cords is about to finish, cut it off and continue with the looping; until you have one cord remaining.
5. Tie the end of this cord very well, so that it will not loosen.
6. Go to the beginning of the cords and cut off the strands there.
7. Fold it to have a length of about eight inches.
8. Use the needle and thread to stitch where the fold was made. Continue with the stitching until you get to the end of the fold. Fold the braided cords over and continue with the stitching.
9. While maintaining a flat work, do this over and over, until you get to the end of the braided cords.
10. At that point, stitch and tighten it securely, so that it will not loosen. Your bathmat is ready to be used.

Macramé Lamp Wire

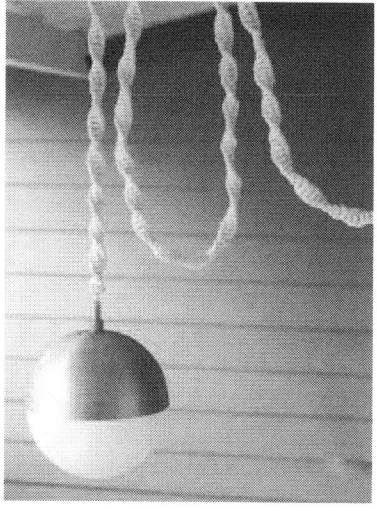

Materials

- Cords

- Scissors

- Lamp with lamp holder

Instructions

1. Measure the length of the cord you want to work on, to determine the length of cord you will use.

2. Cut out your cord and fold it into two.

3. Place it around the cord just before the lamp holder.

4. Take the left side of the cord over to the right and take the right under the cord.

5. Pull the two cords out through the loops.

6. To make it easier for you, fold the left cord over your four fingers to have a big fold. Do the same with the other cord.

7. Take the left one over, and the right one under, and pull each side. Do this again, and you will notice that the pattern will be twisting.

8. Carry on with the pattern until you get to the end of the cable.

9. For the last knot, make a double half-hitch knot, and cut off the remaining cords with your pair of scissors.

Macramé Plant Hanger

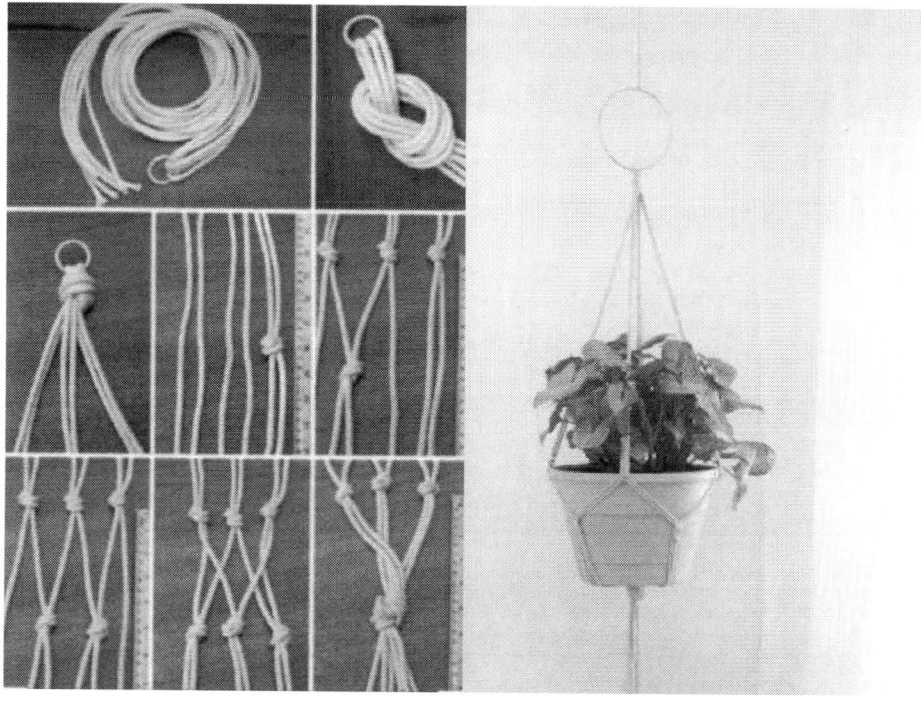

Materials

- 10 long cords

- Ring

- Tape measure

- Scissors

- A macramé boards

Instructions

1. Get eight cords out of the ten and pass them through the ring. Make sure the cords are of equal length and tie them all just after the ring with another cord.

2. Pick four nearest cords and make two left half-square knots, otherwise known as spiral knots.

3. Make the knots until you get the spiral of seven inches in length. After this, leave the cords unplaited and free. The free part should be six inches in length.

4. Make an ocean plait knot and leave the cords to be free for another six inches.

5. Make a two right half-square knots (a spiral knot going towards the right-hand side).

6. Get the other three sets to this level.

7. Now, take two cords from the side you are currently working on, and another two cords from another side, and make a square knot with the cords. The distance between the knots should be seven inches.

8. Take another two cords each from the two sides and entwine them with a square knot. Complete this row.

9. While doing this, the distance between the knots and cords should be even. Continue maintaining the distance, so your work will look good.

10. For the next row, take two cords, each from the two sides, and square knot them. Leaving seven inches, arrange the cords, and tie them together using the remaining cord.

11. Tie the cords carefully and neatly. Leave another seven inches and cut off the extra strands. This is how to make a basic macramé plant hanger.

CHAPTER 9
Macrame Easy and Fun Project 4

Modern Macramé Hanging Planter

Plant hangers are really beautiful because they give your house or garden the feel of an airy, natural space. This one is perfect for condominiums or small apartments— and for those with minimalist, modern themes!

What you need:

- Plant
- Pot
- Scissors
- 50 ft. Paracord (Parachute Cord)
- 16 to 20 mm wooden beads

Instructions:

First, fold in half 4 strands of the cord and then loop so you could form a knot.

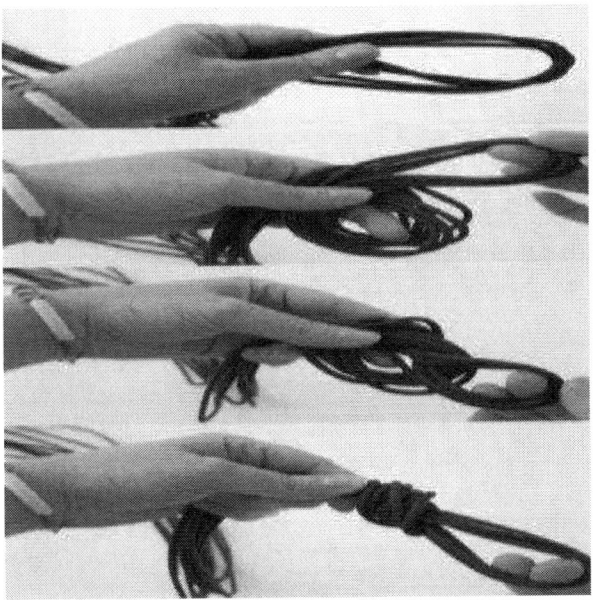

Now, divide the cords into groups of two and make sure to string 2 cords through one of the wooden beads you have on hand. String some more beads—at least 4 on each set of 2 grouped cords.

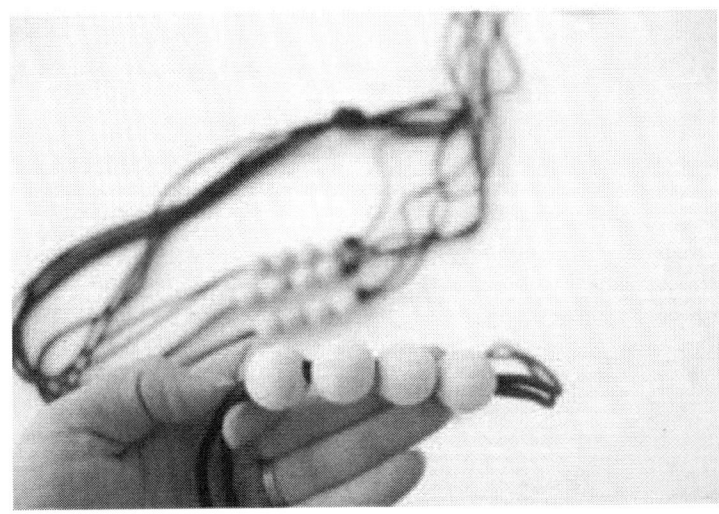

Then, measure every 27.5 inches and tie a knot at that point and repeat this process for every set of cords.

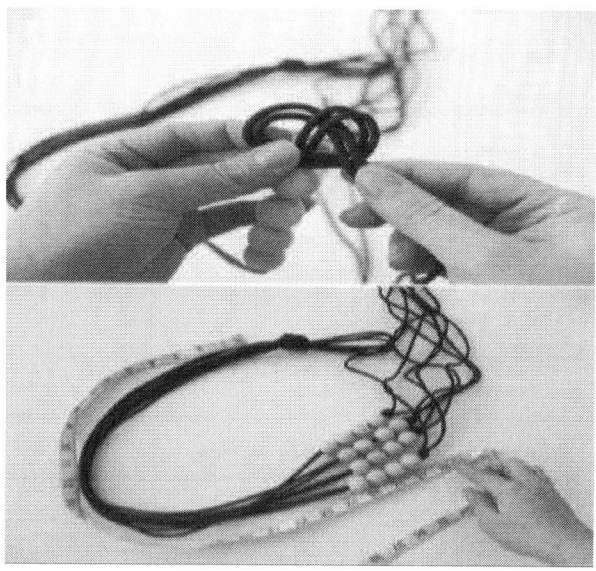

Look at the left set of the cord and tie it to the right string. Repeat on the four sets so that you could make at least 3" from the knot you have made.

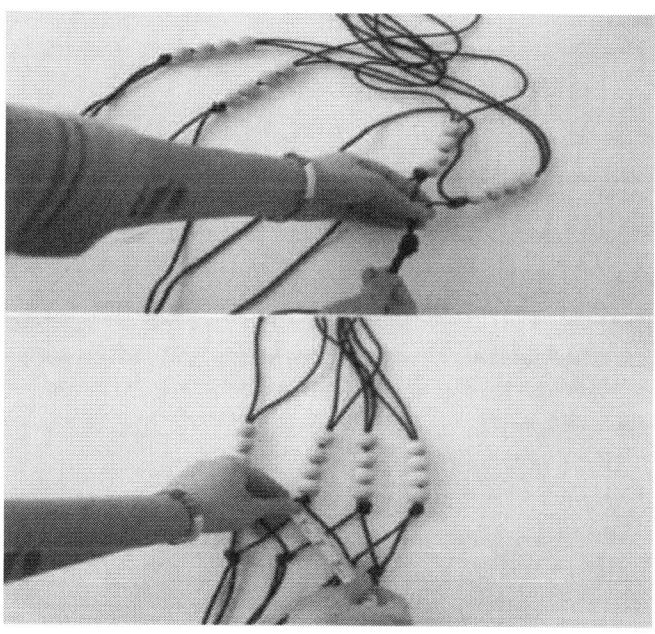

Tie another four knots from the knot that you have made. Make them at least 4.5" each.

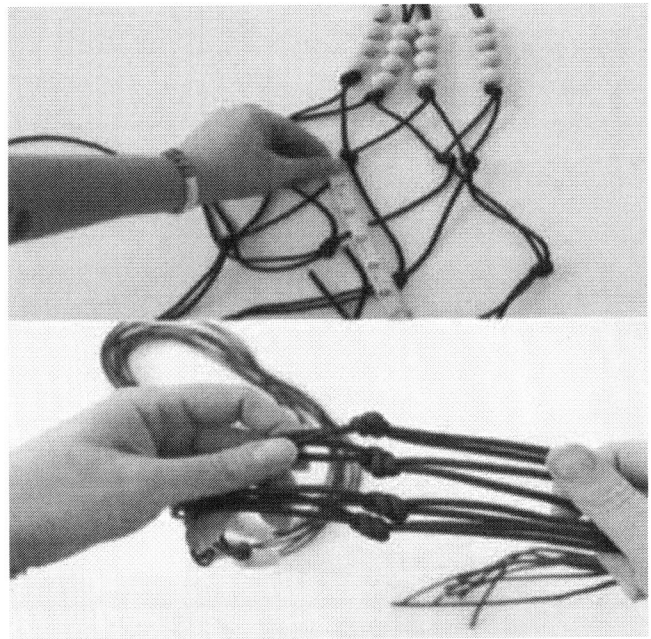

Group all of the cords together and tie a knot to finish the planter. You'll get something like the one shown below—and you could just add your very own planter to it!

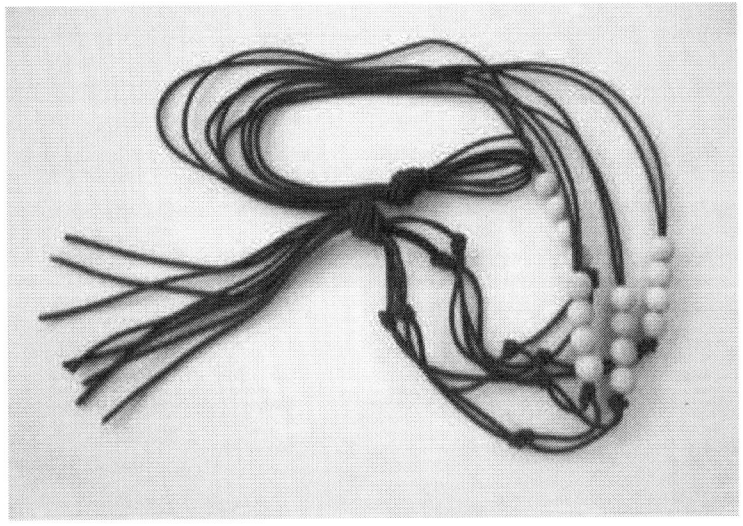

Amazing Macramé Curtain

Macramé Curtains give your house the feel of that beach house look. You don't even have to add any trinkets or shells—but you can, if you want to. Anyway, here's a great macramé Curtain that you can make!

What you need:

- Laundry rope (or any kind of rope/cord you want)
- Curtain rod
- Scissors
- Pins
- Lighter
- tape

Instructions:

Tie four strands together and secure the top knots with pins so they could hold the structure down.

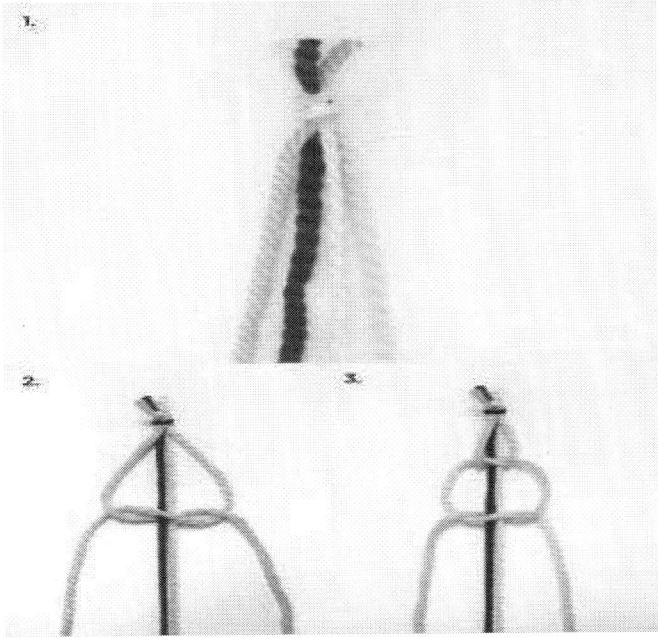

Take the strand on the outer right part and let it cross over to the left side by means of passing it through the middle. Tightly pull the strings together and reverse what you have done earlier.

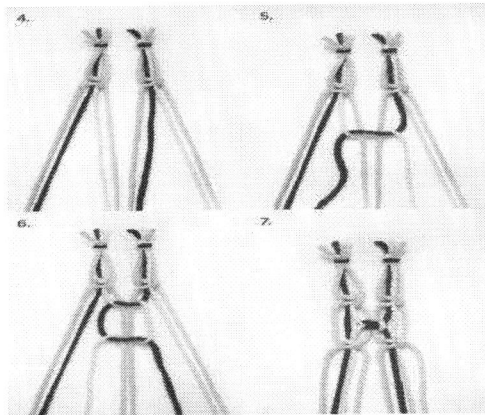

Repeat crossing the thread over four more times for the thread you now have in front of you. Take the strand on the outer left and let it pass through the middle, and then take the right and let it cross over the left side. Repeat as needed, then divide the group of strands to the left, and also to the right. Repeat until you reach the number of rows you want.

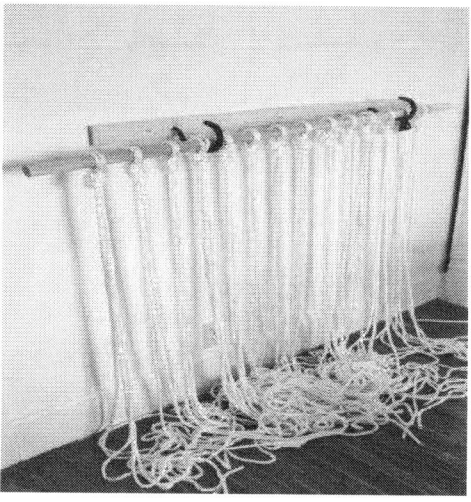

You can now apply this to the ropes. Gather the number of ropes you want—10 to 14 is okay, or whatever fits the rod, with good spacing. Start knotting at the top of the curtain until you reach your desired length. You can burn or tape the ends to prevent them from unraveling.

Braid the ropes together to give them that dreamy, beachside effect, just like what you see below.

That's it, you can now use your new curtain!

Macramé Charm and Feather Décor

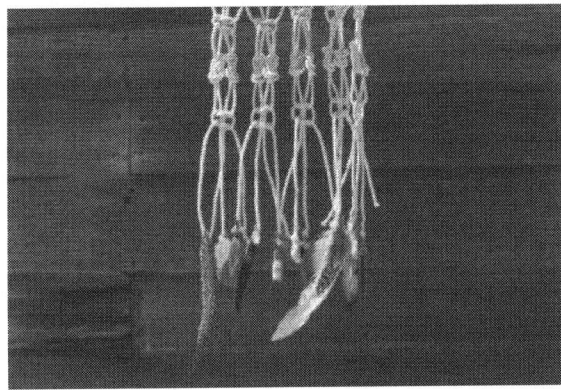

Charms and feathers always look cool. They just add a lot of that enchanting feeling to your house and knowing that you could make macramé décor with charms and feathers really take your crafting game to new heights! Check out the instructions below and try it out for yourself!

What you need:

- Stick/dowel
- feathers and charms with holes (for you to insert the thread in)
- Embroidery/laundry rope (or any other rope or thread that you want)

Instructions:

Cut as many pieces of rope as you want. Around 10 to 12 pieces are good, and then fold each in half. Make sure to create a loop at each end, like the ones you see below:

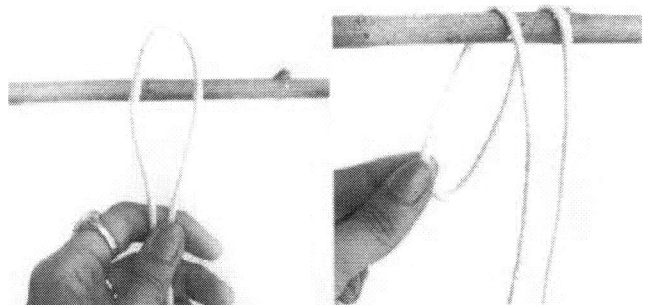

Then, go and loop each piece of thread on the stick.

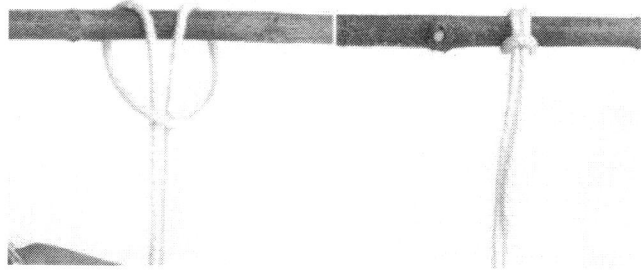

Make use of the square knot and make sure you have four strands for each knot. Let the leftmost strand cross the two strands and then put it over the strands that you have in the middle. Tuck it under the middle two, as well.

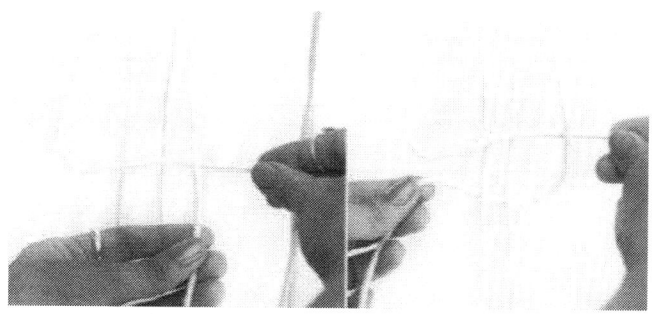

Check under the strands and let the rightmost strand be tucked under the loop to the left-hand strand.

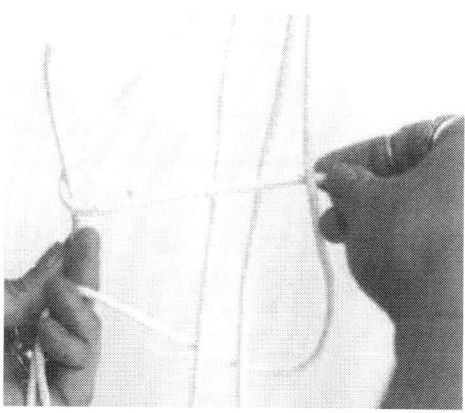

Tighten the loop by pulling the outer strands together and start with the left to repeat the process on the four strands. You will then see that a square knot has formed after tightening the loops together.

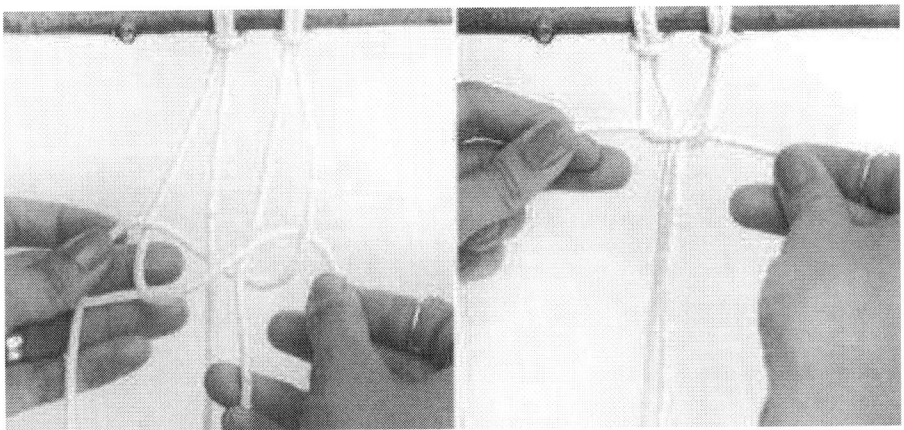

Connect the strands by doing square knots with the remaining four pieces of rope and then repeat the process again from the left side. Tighten the loop by pulling the outer strands together and start with the left to repeat the process on the four strands. You will then see that a square knot has formed after loops have been tightened together.

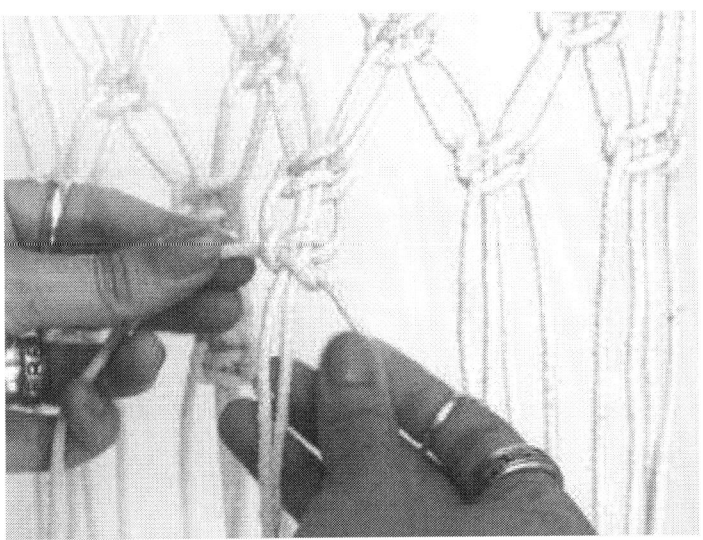

You can then do a figure-eight knot and then just attach charms and feathers to the end. Glue them in and burn the ends for better effect!

Wreath of Nature

Just imagine having a macramé wreath in your home! This one is inspired by nature and is one of the most creative things you could do with your time!

What you need:

- Clips or tape
- Fabric glue
- Wreath or ring frame
- 80 yards 12" cords
- 160 yards 17-18" cords
- 140 yards 14-16" cords
- 120 yards 12-13" cords

Instructions:

Mount the cords on top of the wreath and make the crown knot by folding one of the cords in half. Let the cords pass through the ring and then fold a knot and make sure to place it in front of the ring. Let the loops go over the ring and pull them your way so they could pass the area that has been folded.

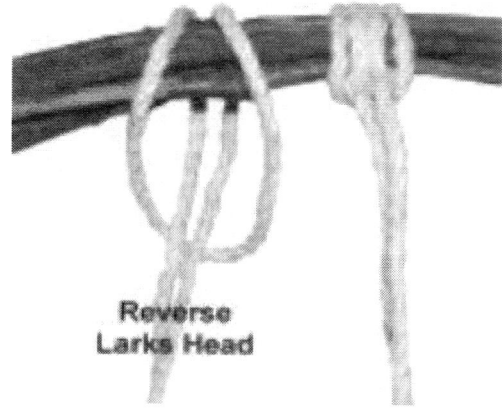

Let the ends pass over the first loop so you could make way for some half-hitches. Let them go over and under the ring, and then tightly pull it over the cord. This way, you'd get something like the one below. Repeat these first few steps until you have mounted all the cords on top of the ring. Organize them in groups of ten.

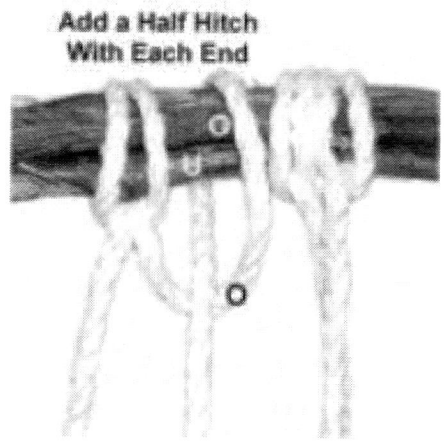

Now, you can make leaf-like patterns. To do this, make sure to number the first group of cords on the right side and make half-hitches in a counterclockwise direction. Take note that you have to horizontally place the holding plate. If you see that it has curved slightly, make sure to reposition it and then attach cords labeled 5 to 7. Move it to resemble a diagonal position and then attach cords 8 to 10.

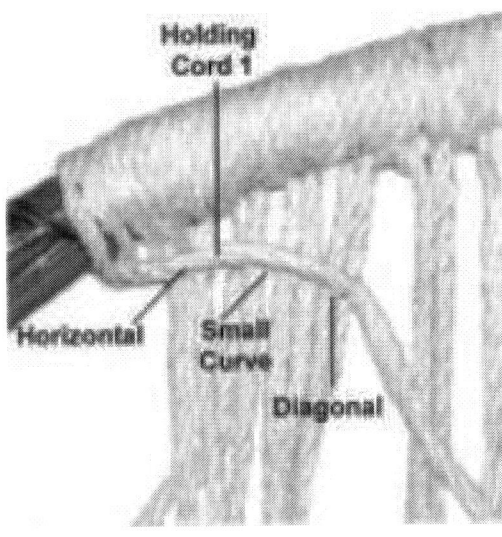

Make sure knots have been pushed close together and then use the cord on the leftmost corner to lower the leaf-like portion. The first four cords should be together on the handle and then go and attach cords labeled 3 to 6 to the holding cord. Move the cords so they'd be in a horizontal position.

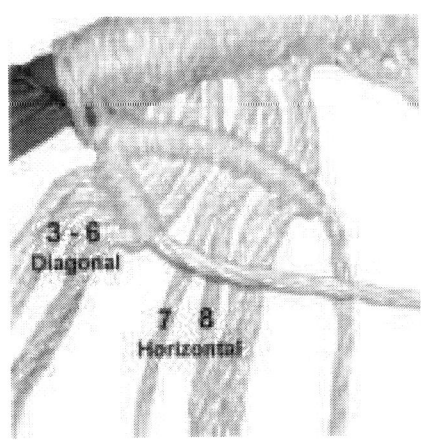

Now, move the cord upwards so that the center would not curve unnecessarily. Repeat the process for the cords on the bottom part of the frame and then start making the branches by selecting 2 to 4 cords from each of the leaves. Don't select the first and second row's first and last leaves.

Hold the cords with tape or clips as you move them towards the back of the design and decide how you want to separate—or keep the branches together. Secure the cords with glue after moving them to the back.

Wrap the right cords around the ones on the left so that branches could be joined together. Make sure to use half-hitches to wrap this portion and then use a set of two cords to create a branch.

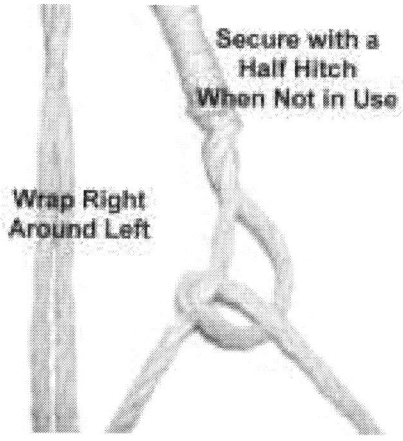

Let the branches intertwine by checking the plan you have written earlier and then use half-hitches again to connect the branches together. Together with your wrap, make use of another wrap and make sure they all come together as one.

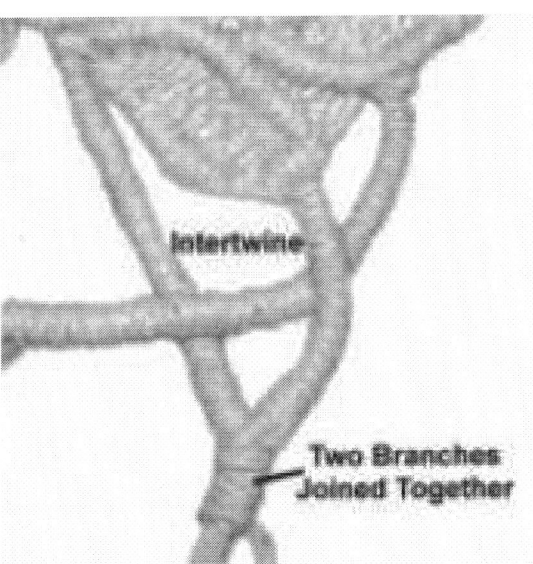

Secure the bundle by wrapping a 3-inch wrap cord around it and then let it go over the completed knot.

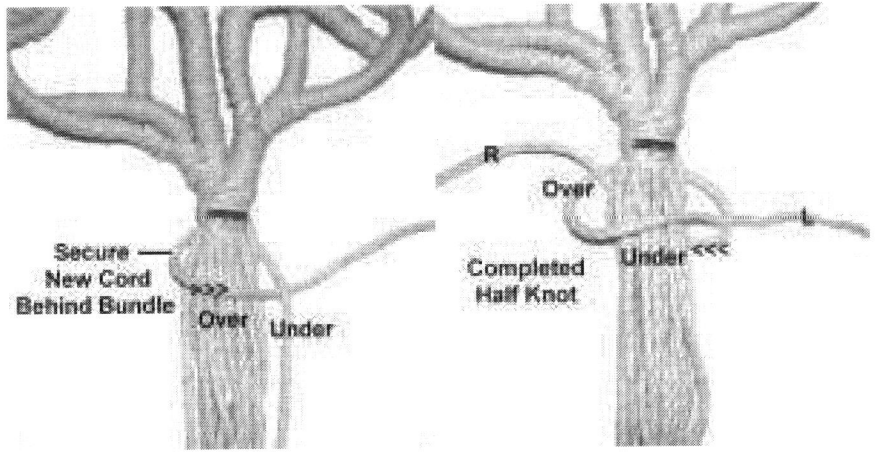

As for the fringe, you have to divide the knots into groups of two and make sure to tie a half-hitch on the rightmost cord on the leftover, and then let them alternate back and forth continuously until you have managed to cover the whole wreath. Let each sennit slide under the whole wreath and then attach each cord to the ring itself.

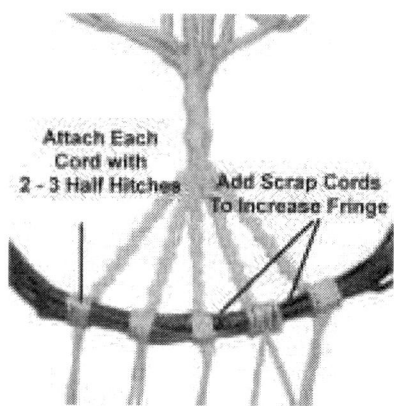

Make sure to divide the cords into small groups and then use the cords so you could tie the overhand knots. Unravel the fibers so you could form a wavy fringe.

That's it! You now have your own macramé Wreath of Nature!

Macramé Skirt Hanger

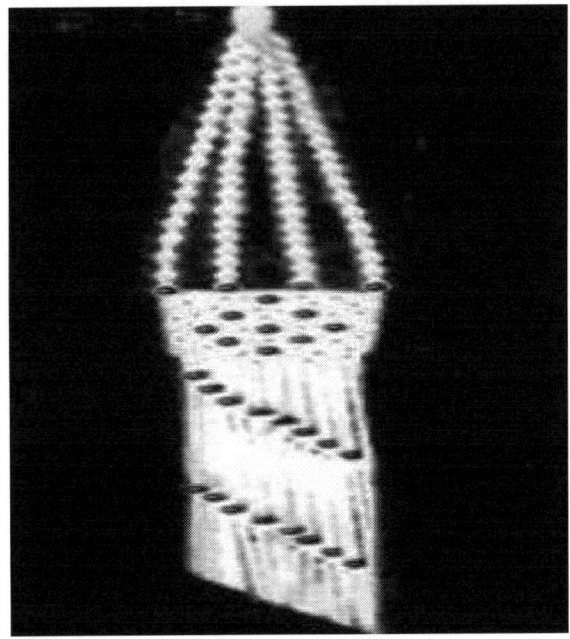

Well, it's not really a skirt hanger. But it's something that could spruce up your closet or your walls. It gives the room that dainty, airy feeling. You could also use it for plant pots that are at least 8 inches in size.

What you need:

- 12 mm size beads
- Onc 8-inch ring
- One 2-inch ring
- 4mm cord

Instructions:

First, cut 8 cords that are at least 8.5 yards long then cut a cord that is 36 inches long before cutting 4 more yards of cord.

Then, fold the 8.5 yards in half to start the top of the thread. Let it pass through the ring and let some parts drape down before choosing two cords from outside the bundle. Make sure to match the ends and then try the square knot.

To bundle the locks, you should find the center and move 8 inches down from it and then stop when you reach 12 inches.

Wrap the center a couple of times and then pull the ends tightly until you build a sturdy bundle, and then tug on the ends so that the roll could get smaller.

Make a total of four spirals that could at least be 20 inches and then manage the filler cords by adding a bead to them. To make the basket, attach the cords to the 8-inch ring by using double half-hitch stitches and then arrange the cords so they could be in four groups. Pull the stitches tightly so there's enough space and then mount all of the cords to the ring in a counterclockwise motion. To cover the ring, make sure to tie a half-hitch at each end.

Then, make alternating square knots just below the ring and divide into two groups of 40 strings each—it sounds like a lot but it's what would naturally happen. Add some tape to the cords you have labeled 1 to 40 and then tie a half-square knot to the four injected threads. Add some beads, and then tie a knot again.

Add beads to cords 20 to 21 after using cords 19 to 22 and then make alternating square knots and then repeat on the cords on the backside. Add beads and make more alternating square knots, then add beads to cords 16 to 17 after using cords labeled 15 to 18. Tie the row without adding any beads and then use cords 11 to 30. Work on cords 12 to 29 by adding beads to them and making use of alternating square knots. Repeat the 3rd row with no beads, and the 4th row with beads, and choose four of your favorite cords to make fringes.

Speaking of fringes, number the remaining cords mentally and then add a succession of 2 to 3 beads for each layer (i.e., 2/4/6 or 3/6/9) and then trim all the cords evenly.

Enjoy your new Skirt Hanger!

CHAPTER 10
Macrame Easy and Fun Project 5

Macramé Tassel Earring

The most effective method to make macramé tassel earrings We're currently getting into one of my preferred macramé projects – hoops! All the more explicitly, tassel hoops. In case you're hoping to get some motivation and ideas for your next macramé project, look no further as macramé earrings are an incredible apprentice amicable project you can rapidly begin with.

Materials Needed:

- 3mm Cotton Cord
- Weaving String
- Earrings
- Length of Cotton Cord:
- 6 x (3" –5") threads (for one hoop)
- Length of Embroidery String:
- 1 x 22" (for one earring)

Macramé earrings are easy to make and are ideal for any event. You can wear them as a fashion statement, blending and coordinating with different accessories. It is a great method to show your exceptional style and artistry. I appreciate making macramé earrings. Therefore, for this macramé project, you will spend around 45 min–1 hour to make them. You will utilize just two knots for this project—a twofold half knot ties an overhand tie. You will no doubt need to get yourself some macramé string and a couple of band earrings for this project.

If earrings interest you, be certain you give this macramé DIY project a go!

Macramé Coaster

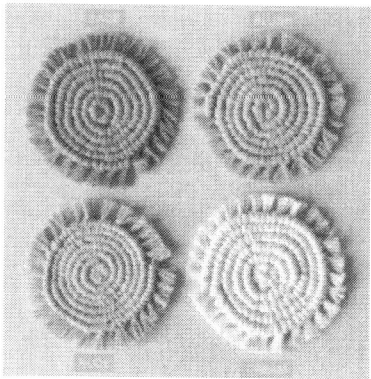

Hoping to add some DIY home, stylistic theme to your living space? Have a go at making this adorable little macramé coaster!

Macramé coaster is an extraordinary beginner DIY project for anybody hoping to begin on their first barely any macramé projects. This project will fill you 2 needs.

- Help invigorate your imagination.

- It is reasonable and can be utilized.

Macramé Materials Needed:

- 4mm Single Strand Cotton Cord

- Stitch Hook

- Lengths of Cord

- 3 x 170cm 1 x 50cm

This is an incredible macramé project thought in case you're hoping to make something reasonably without any problem. It's superb for those hoping to begin with macramé or the individuals who simply need to make some macramé liners. As a heads up, in case you're anticipating causing this napkin, to know it can get somewhat dubious with regards to knotting and knotting in a round shape. You will discover when working in a circular shape and you will frequently be required to continually turn and move the project around the task while you are knotting. It can get somewhat befuddling on occasion, yet with some training; you ought to have the option to easily float through the creation of these liners in a matter of moments. For this task, you may be required to know 2 knots–the lark's head knot and twofold half knot tie. The estimated time for this project is 60 minutes.

Mini Pumpkin Macrame Hanger

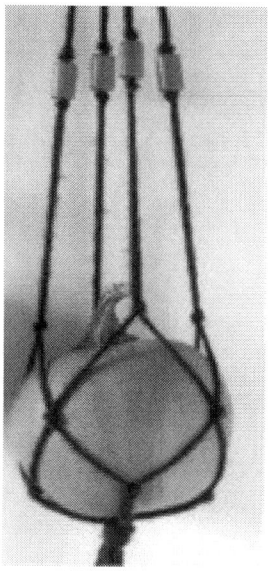

Supplies:

- Black thread or line.
- Metal loop.
- Hollow pearls
- Scissors

Instructions:

Cut 4 yarn strands about 3 times the completed hanger length. Fold the threads in the middle of the metal hoop.

The yarn strands are then divided into two groups. Connect a knot to each group. Cord a wooden bead on each thread, then tie another knot just below the bead. Join a pair of knots a couple of inches apart. Then tie two neighboring strings together and repeat each string. Then tie with the first line the last line. Continue this process and bring another string together. Finally, tie all the strings in a large knot.

Bohemian Macrame Mirror Wall Hanging

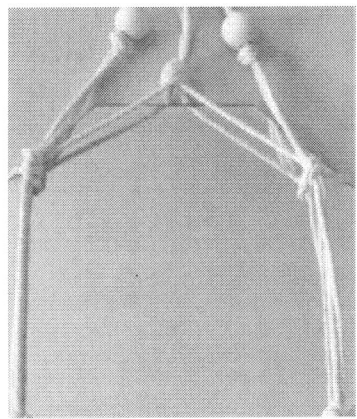

Supplies:

- Macrame cord: 4 mm

- Octagon Mirror

- Ring of wood: 2

- Wood Beads: Size Hole 25 mm w/10 mm

- Sharp Scissors

- Macrame Mirror Model

Instructions:

Cut 4 bits of Macrame into 108 inches (or 3yds).

Macrame Larks Mirror Knot

Bend the strips in half and tie all 4 of them on the wooden cord with a head knot of Lark. Tighten the ties and lock them. Divide the two knots of the Lark 's Head into a knot square.

Square Knot Macrame Mirror Model

Tie together two knots.

Begin tie two cubic knots into Lark's second two head knots.

Mirror macrame knot square

When the second knot is started, bend it to one side of the other two knots to merge it into a big knot.

Tie 7 knots square running on each side and on all sides.

Macrame square knot creator

After the knots are joined, break the ends. Two strings on both hand and four strings in the middle. Place the string on the ends to show the broken ends. This makes it easier to add the beads. Thanks! It is the most difficult part! The rest connects only basic knots and even gets on the sides.

Add macrame perforations. Place one bead on both hands. Place a knot on both sides under the bead to hold it even. Tie 4 strings in the middle or about 1/14 centimeter below the beads.

Macrame mirror beaded, macrame mirror, white macrame mirror simple knotted.

Take a single cord from the middle and attach it to the 2 cords on the ends. Bind the three on both sides in a knot. Connect the mirror even to the knot lengths. Attach one of the three side cords to the mirror back to keep it steady.

Easy knots in all three cords at the left and right bottom of the mirror. Separate the three cords again. Put one on both sides of the mirror to place two on the front of the mirror and tie in a knot.

Knots on macrame mirror back, basic mirror macrame technology.

Flip the mirror over and tie all the cords together. Flip the mirror over and loosen the front knot. Glide into the knot the back cords and straighten the knot. Cut the cord to around 14 inches. Pull the ends or loosen the strings and let the ends go. Combine a smooth comb with the ends of the thread. Hang and go!

Macramé Feathers

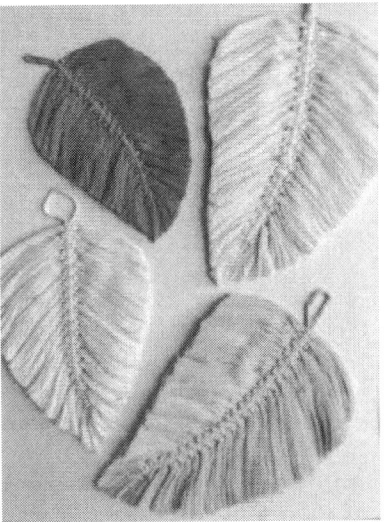

If you're hoping to improve your macramé projects with more details and texture, there's no preferred path over by including feathers. You can likewise transform the feathers into straightforward key chains, hoops, charms or other jewelry also.

Macramé Supplies Needed:

- 4mm Single Strand Cotton Cord

- Treated steel brush

- Estimating Tape

- Lengths of Cord:

- Feathers #1 (11cm wide, 14cm height)

- 1 x 40cm Strand

- 14 x (13-15cm) Strands

- Feathers Tassel #2 (11cm wide, 14cm height)

- 1 x 90cm Strand

- 1 x 150cm Strand

- 14 x (13-15cm) Strand

- Feathers #3 (11cm wide, 14cm height)

- 1 x 30cm Strand

- 1 x 80cm Strand

- 8 x (13-15cm) Strand

For this fledgling DIY macramé project, I will share three contrast macramé feathers that you can use to consolidate into your greater macramé projects or make it a feather charm.

Macramé feathers stand apart because of its fluffy fringe and texture. It's troublesome not to stop and take a second look when you see a macramé project brightened with feathers and leaves. Many respects the feathers and leaves on a piece and are fascinated to figure out how to make them sooner or later in their macramé project.

If you're hoping to say something with your macramé structures and projects, there's no preferred path over with macramé feathers and leaves. To figure out how to make these feathers, you will require the accompanying supplies and track within the instructional exercise beneath. Feel free to check it out!

Macramé DIY Garlands

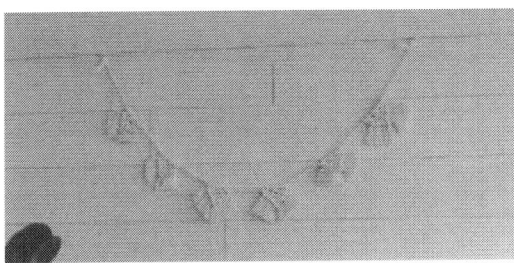

Materials needed:

- macramé yarn
- sharp scissors
- wood beads
- hair comb (if you want to brush out the edges)

You have to knot two tiny pieces of macramé completely and make for the correct length of garland.

So, when you create one piece of macramé between any of these wood beads you have to cut 6 pieces of 40-inch macramé string that you have to replicate twice or as large you like your garland to be. You may need to cut 13 pieces of 40-inch strings of macramé yarn.

Begin the novice macramé garland by folding the 40-inch macramé parts in half and looping them with Lark's Head Knots onto the baseline.

Take them close, then repeat them 6 times.

You have to do square knots after that. Differentiate that string that is placed on top. You have to balance the knots after creating a chain so that you can build a pyramid at the top. So, it is time to create Half-hitch triangular ties on either hand of the small triangle macramé. Such forms of knots are essential loops put on either side of the outer rope and then intersect in the center of the line. So, it almost ends the garland. You may either opt to keep the garland free or at the bottom, you may tie off any macramé into a little tassel.

Macramé DIY Bag

The more you practice the faster you get and I have to admit we enjoyed blowing off some steam creating macramé rope packs, making fun and (luckily) oh-so on-trend right now! While knotting!

You Need:

- String
- Scissors
- Two Gold Jump-Ring
- Needle and Thread

A little thought, we did both a macramé brace and a macramé knotted bag segment for this one. That said, if you just choose to do the portion of the knotted case, you can only add a leather band to the gold rings. Completely up to you!

To make the handle, start by knotting the bag string. That half of the rope would need to be knotted individually and the duration of each piece of string will be half the total duration of the band, times 4. As an example, the strings may reach a minimum of 45 cm (18 inches) and the bits of string that were cut were half the amount 4. Split the string in two, then use the folded end to tie it on your rope. Apply 4 ties. Take the inner string and wrap it around the outer string, beginning with the knot at the top. You need to tighten your knot. Then, repeat the prior knot, this time just with the next line. Knot the other side of the straps utilizing the same form of knotting, this time inverting the path only. Do it 5 times on both sides. Now connect the two strands by stretching the ties using the same knotting process. Repeat three times on those extended sets. Instead change the course and tie for the next three sides from left to right. Do the side ties once again. Once you've achieved so, half the brace is over! Do this with the other brace and rope and then attach. Do the same knot again to complete the knot work. Snip off one of the threads in the knot then use the next strand to start forming a fresh knot. Line up the ends and tie together with needle and thread to fasten the belts on.

Build the interior of the rope bag and make the main part of your pocket, cut ten pieces of string which are four times the length of the bag you like. The rope bag body is made using package ties. Taking two strings to the hand, thread the two middle threads around it. Do the loop again, then secure the tie. Repeat the knots on the remaining threads, remember to keep the lengths between the knots and the hoops close. For the second row proceed to do box loops, using only one string over this period. Knot three rows of box ties on both ends, use two strands from either side until knotting the edges of the container. Continue to do box ties until the scale of the bag is the one that you like. When you don't want any tassel ends, snip off the ends of the loops and rub a little glue into the ties to seal them. Flip your bag open.

CHAPTER 11
Terminologies

Of course, you could also expect that there are certain terms you would be dealing with while trying Macramé out. By knowing these terms, it would be easier for you to make Macramé projects. You won't have a hard time, and the crafting will be a breeze!

For this, you should keep the following in mind!

Alternating

This is applied to patterns where more than one cord is being tied together. It involves switching and looping, just like the half-hitch.

Adjacent

These are knots or cords that rest to one another.

Alternating Square Knots (ASK)

You'll find this in most Macramé patterns. As the name suggests, it's all about square knots that alternate on a fabric.

Bar

When a distinct area is raised in the pattern, it means that you have created a "bar". This could either be diagonal, horizontal, or vertical.

Band

A design that has been knotted to be flat or wide.

Buttonhole (BH)

This is another name given to the Crown or Lark's head knot. It has been used since the Victorian Era.

Button Knot

This is a knot that is firm and is round.

Bundle

These are cords that have been grouped as one. They could be held together by a knot.

Braided Cord

These are materials with individual fibers that are grouped as one. It is also stronger than most materials because all the fibers work together as one.

Braid

Sometimes called Plait, this describes 3 or more cords that have been woven under or over each other.

Body

This talks about the projects.

Bight

This is in the thread that has carefully been folded so loops could also make their way out to the knots.

Crook

This is just the part of the loop that has been curved and is situated near the crossing point.

Core

This term refers to a group of cords that are running along the center of a knot. They're also called "filling cords".

Cord

This could either be the material, or cord/thread that you are using, or specific cords that have been designed to work together.

Combination Knot

These are two knots that have been designed to work as one.

Cloisonné

A bead with metal filaments that are used for decorative purposes.

Chinese Crown Knot

This is usually used for Asian-inspired jewelry or décor.

Charm

This is a small bead that is meant to dangle and is usually just an inch in size.

Doubled

These are patterns that have been repeated in a single pattern.

Double Half Hitch (DHH)

This is a specific type of knot that's not used in a lot of crafts, except for really decorative, unusual ones. This is made by making sure that two half hitches are resting beside each other.

Diameter

This describes the material's weight, based on millimeters.

Diagonal

This is a row of knots or cord that runs from the upper left side to the opposite.

Excess Material

This describes the part of the thread that's left hanging after you have knotted the fabric. Sometimes, it's hidden using fringes, too.

Fusion Knots

This starts with a knot so you could make a new design.

Fringe

This is a technique that allows cords to dangle down with individual fibers that unravel themselves along with the pattern.

Flax Linen

This is material coming from Linseed Oil that's best used for making jewelry, and even Macramé clothing—it has been used for over 5000 years already.

Finishing Knot

This is a kind of knot that allows specific knots to be tied to the cords so they would not unravel.

Findings

These are closures for necklaces or other types of jewelry.

Gemstone Chips

This is the term given to semi-precious stones that are used to decorate or embellish your Macramé projects. The best ones are usually quartz, jade, or turquoise.

Horizontal

This is a design of the cord that works from left to the right.

Holding Cord

This is the cord where the working cords are attached to.

Hitch

This is used to attach cords to cords, dowels, or rings.

Inverted

This means that you are working on something "upside-down".

Interlace

This is a pattern that could be woven or intertwined so different areas could be linked together.

Micro-Macramé

This is the term given to Macramé projects that are quite small.

Metallic

These are materials that resemble silver, brass, or gold.

Mount

Mount or Mounting means that you have to attach a cord to a frame, dowel, or ring and is usually done at the start of a project.

Netting

This is a process of knotting that describes knots formed between open rows of space and is usually used in wall hangings, curtains, and hammocks.

Natural

These are materials made from plants or plant-based materials. Examples include hemp, Jude, and flax.

Organize

This is another term given to cords that have been collected or grouped as one.

Picot

These are loops that go through the edge of what you have knotted.

Pendant

A décor that you could add to a necklace or choker and could easily fit through the loops.

Synthetic

This means that the material you are using is man-made, and not natural.

Symmetry

This means that the knots are balanced.

Standing End

This is the end of the cord that you have secured so the knot would be properly constructed.

Texture

This describes how the cord feels like in your hand.

Tension or Taut

This is the term given to holding cords that have been secured or pulled straight so that they would be tighter than the other working cords.

Vertical

This describes knots that have been knotted upwards, or in a vertical manner.

Working End

This is the part of the cord that is used to construct the knot.

Weave

This is the process of letting the cords move as you let them pass over several segments in your pattern.

Conclusion

There you have it, everything you need to know to get you started with your own macramé knots. This is going to show you just how easy it is to get started in this hobby, and once you get the hang of things, you are going to find that it is easier than ever to start with your own projects.

Macramé is an enjoyable craft to try, and with a limited budget, you can continue. There are plenty of free or affordable patterns and some great ways to get books started. That would be a great craft to include your kids, grandkids, or anyone else.

Determining a period to learn macramé will depend on many factors, such as how quickly the technology is acquired. If you have been weaving or sewing for a long time, the degree of complexity should be much lower because of the similarities of the methods.

Let's use it to display our plants for a more natural touch at home, workplace, exhibition, etc. If you love art, there are many opportunities to learn to trade and shop beautifully.

As you have read this book, do not simply discard it. Keep it as a guide and look out for more extensive materials online and offline to help you perfect your skills. This book explains basic knots and projects for beginners, but if you practice Macramé regularly, you wouldn't be a beginner for long. Macramé can be very relaxing, and it is an amazing avenue to bring family and friends together. As you have learnt here, you can teach your loved ones some of these basic knots and refer them to obtain their copy of this carefully prepared beginner's guide to Macramé.

Macramé has changed ... yes, it's all part of the creative cycle that endures on several levels. Both experienced macramé artisans and experts consider it relaxing, enjoyable, imaginative, and satisfying. There are more and more options for superior macramé to improve the decor of your house, wardrobe and personal style for those who just want to use and enjoy the finished pieces to decide a period of time it will take to learn how to macramé depends on various factors such as how easily you will learn this technique. If you have been knitting or sewing for a long time, the degree of difficulty will be slightly lower, as there are some parallels with the process. There you have it, well done, everything you need to know to get you started with your own macramé knots. You learned just how easy it is to get started in this hobby, and once you get the hang of things, you are going to find that it is easier than ever to get started with your own projects.

Remember that each of these knots will be the foundation of the other projects you create, so you are going to have to take the time to get familiar with each of them—and practice them until they are what you need them to be. You are not likely going to get them perfectly right away—so take the time to make sure you do it right before you move on to the succeeding one.

Do not worry if you do not get it at first it is going to come with time, and the more time you put into it, the better you are going to become. It does take time and effort to get it right, but the more time and effort you put into it, the better you are going to be. My goal with this is to give you the inspiration and direction you need to master macramé.

It can be difficult at first, but the more you put into it, the easier it is all going to become until it is just second nature to you. I know you are going to fall in love with each and every aspect of this hobby, and when you know how to work the knots, you are going to want to make them in all the ways you possibly can.

Do not worry about the colors, and do not worry if you do not get it right the first time. This is going to give you everything you need to make it happen the way you want it to, and it is going to show you that you really can have it all with your macramé projects.

I hope you become a master at this hobby and that you can get the projects you want from the patterns you use. There is no end to the ways you can create macramé projects, and the more familiar you become with them, the easier it is going to be for you to make them no matter what you want them to be. So, dive into the world of macramé with both feet, and learn that there is nothing that is going to stand in your way when it comes to these projects. So, what are you waiting for? All it is going to take is your time and effort, and you are going to get just what you are after with your macramé projects. From now on, you are on the path to be a macramé master, and you are going to fall in love with everything macramé. The world of macramé awaits, just begging you to dive in and get started.

Stop reading; start doing!

Printed in Great Britain
by Amazon

63867336R00079